# BASEBALL'S
## STRANGEST
## MOMENTS

# BASEBALL'S STRANGEST MOMENTS

## ROBERT OBOJSKI

Drawings by Sandy Hoffman

 **Sterling Publishing Co., Inc.   New York**

## Other Books of Interest

Baseball Brain Teasers
Baseball: Startling Stories Behind the Records
Baseball's Strangest Moments
Guinness Sports Record Book
Youth League Baseball

**LIBRARY OF CONGRESS**
Library of Congress Cataloging-in-Publication Data

Obojski, Robert.
    Baseball's strangest moments / Robert Obojski ; drawings by Sandy
Hoffman.
        p.   cm.
    Includes index.
    Summary: True stories of events on and off the baseball field
highlighting some unusual or unique aspects about players,
executives, rules, and customs.
    ISBN 0-8069-4194-4.   ISBN 0-8069-4195-2 (lib. bdg.)
    1. Baseball--United States--History--Juvenile literature.
[1. Baseball--History.]   I. Hoffman, Sanford, ill.   II. Title.
GV863.A1O27 1988
796.357'0973--dc19                                          87-33319
                                                                 CIP
                                                                  AC

Published by Sterling Publishing Co., Inc.
Two Park Avenue, New York, N.Y. 10016
Distributed in Canada by Oak Tree Press Ltd.
% Canadian Manda Group, P.O. Box 920, Station U
Toronto, Ontario, Canada M8Z 5P9
Distributed in the United Kingdom by Blandford Press
Link House, West Street, Poole, Dorset BH15 1LL, England
Distributed in Australia by Capricorn Ltd.
P.O. Box 665, Lane Cove, NSW 2066
*Manufactured in the United States of America*
Sterling ISBN 0-8069-4194-4 Trade
                    4195-2 Library

4

# ABOUT THE AUTHOR

Robert Obojski as a youth was an inveterate sandlot baseball player and worked his way through college by handling a number of part-time jobs with the Cleveland Indians—as groundskeeper first, then operator of the electric scoreboard, and eventually as statistician for the baseball telecasts.

Over the years he has written many hundreds of articles on all phases of baseball, in addition to three full-length books: *Bush League—A History of Minor League Baseball* (Macmillan, 1975), *The Rise of Japanese Baseball Power* (Chilton, 1975), and *All-Star Baseball Since 1933* (Stein & Day, 1980).

Obojski is also a well-known hobby writer, credited with a number of books on numismatics and philately, including: *Ships and Explorers on Coins* (Sterling, 1970), *An Introduction to Stamp Collecting* (Dover, 1984), *Coin Collector's Price Guide* (Sterling, 1986), *Stamp Collector's Price Guide* (Sterling, 1986), and co-author of *An Illustrated Encyclopedia of World Coins* (Doubleday, 1970; rev. ed., 1983).

He currently serves as a contributing editor to a variety of magazines, including: *Collector Editions Quarterly, Miniature Collector, Dolls Magazine,* and *Teddy Bear Review.* He is also a contributing editor to the *Guinness Book of World Records* and the *Guinness Sports Record Book.*

# DEDICATION

This book is dedicated to the late great Dick Young, a brilliant writer who spent nearly a half-century covering sports—baseball in particular—for the *New York Daily News* and later for the *New York Post*. Dick was an absolutely fearless writer who always had the courage of his convictions and who never backed off from discussing controversial issues and controversial personalities.

Dick Young was a man of boundless energy who traveled enormous distances in order to cover major sports events staged around the country and around the world. He was never content to write about a game or a match from a mere press box vantage point. Rather, after the last out or the last point was made, he'd rush down to the locker rooms to interview the key participants. Thus, in pioneering the post-game, post-match interview, Dick was able to convey to his readers graphically the feel of the blood and sweat of the battle.

Dick, your millions of readers are going to miss you, especially those of us who've ever tried to write about sports.

ROBERT OBOJSKI

# ACKNOWLEDGMENTS

Special thanks go to Thomas R. Heitz, Librarian at the National Baseball Hall of Fame and Museum, Cooperstown, New York, for assisting us in locating elusive bits of information necessary for the completion of this book.

Thanks also to Bob Fishel, Executive Vice President of the American League, who is always kind enough to answer questions and supply information.

Moreover, my wife, Danuta, a professional librarian, has a certain knack for tracking down bits of baseball esoterica squirreled away in old newspapers and magazines.

Finally, we must give due credit to David A. Boehm, chairman of the Sterling Publishing Co. and a serious student of baseball, who helped conceive this project.

# CONTENTS

INTRODUCTION—Baseball, A Strange Career   10

1. STRANGE EVENTS
   On Mother's Day, Feller's Mother Struck by Foul Ball   13
   Strange Pinch Hitter Draws Roars with Outrageous Stunt   15
   Don't Roll That Tarpaulin—Coleman Might Be Inside!   17
   Tebbetts Crowned by Basket of Tomatoes in "Vegetable
      War"   18
   Two Balls in Play at Same Time—An Umpire's Mental
      Lapse   22
   Jackie Robinson Got Minimum Salary—$5,000 When Rickey
      Brought Him to Big Leagues   23
   Hit a Homer in Japan and Win a Sword   24
   Is Big League Baseball Ready for Lady Umpires?   26
   Get the X-ray Machines Ready! No Cork in the Bats
      Please!   28
   "Dead" Balls, Lop-Sided Balls—They Were All Playable
      Then   30
   Autograph Hunters Are Dangerous to a Player's Health!   32
   Wild Throws Can Be Dangerous   33
   Hit on Head by Bat While in On-Deck Circle   33
   "Stone Age" Gave Fans Plenty of Excitement   34
   Centerfielder Carlisle Makes Unassisted Triple Play   37
   The Day Cobb and Sisler Were Mound Opponents   38
   Cramer and Williams: A Classic Collision in the
      Outfield   38
   Strange Game in Cuba: Gunfire Around the Ball Park   39

2. STRANGE PLAYERS
   Piersall Clubs 100th Homer, Runs Bases Backwards   41
   From Big League Ballplayer to Evangelist: Billy Sunday   41
   The Strange Case of Alan "Inky" Strange   47
   The Strange Case of Pete Gray, One-Armed Outfielder   48
   "Goofy" Gomez Stops Pitching in World Series to Watch
      Passing Airplane   50
   Yogi Berra Strikes Out Three Times, "Not Nowhere" Will He
      Play Like That   51
   Rose's Strange Retirement from Active Play   52
   Strange Batting Style Leads Oh to Home Run Hitting
      Record   53

Catchers Are a Strange Breed: Lopez, Boone and Bateman
Prime Examples  54
Bobo Newsom Disdains Perfume  56

3. STRANGE EXECUTIVES
Owner Steinbrenner, Baseball's Dr. Jekyll and Mr. Hyde  57
Bill Veeck: Baseball's Showman Extraordinaire  59
Game Bores Manager—Leaves Bench for Hot Dog  63
Turner Manages His Braves for One Day  64
Walt Alston Goes Down Swinging in His Only At-Bat in
Majors  67
From Boswell to Baseball: The Case of President
Giamatti  68

4. TOUGH PITCHERS
Nolan Ryan: King of Zing  70
Fastest Pitcher? Ryan 100.9 MPH, Dalkowski 108  71
Spitball Pitcher Spat in Umpire's Face!  72
George Blaeholder, Father of the Slider  74
Pitches for 23 Teams in 13 Leagues During a 27-Year
Career  75
It Didn't Pay to Mess with Burly Early Wynn  76

5. TOUGH BATTERS
Ty Cobb: Long Ball Hitter and Tiger on the Base Paths  77
Joe Sewell: "Iron Man," A Tough Batter to Strike Out  79
Pete Rose: Slugger Began at Age 3, Wasted Valuable Years in
High School  81
Babe Ruth: Beats Whole American League in Home Run
Production  83
Jimmie Foxx and Mickey Mantle: Who Hit Ball Harder?  84
Joe DiMaggio: Always One Tough Hombre to Strike Out  86
Johnny Mize and Ted Williams: Very Tough to Strike Out  87
Bill Dickey: Didn't Take Many Third Strikes Either  88
"Shoeless" Joe Jackson: More Triples Than Strikeouts  88
Don Mattingly: Hits with Extra Oomph, Sets Two Homer
Records in 1987  89
Reggie Jackson: King of the Whiffers  90
Baseballs Travel Like Rockets—Can Even Scare Veteran
Players  91

6. THE STRANGE DH RULE
Pitcher Was Such a Terrible Batter He Brought On the DH
Rule  94

First (Illegal) Use of a Designated Hitter   95
Bob Buhl Goes 0 for 70   96
Relief Pitchers Need Relief at Bat   97
Still a Regular at 44—Yaz Sets Mark for Long Career   98
Extend the DH Rule to Both Leagues   100


7. WEAK HITTERS AND BIG LOSERS
Scott Sets Consecutive Game Record Before Being Benched
for Weak Hitting   102
Del Ennis Leaves 500 Stranded—Clean-Up Hitter Can't Clean
Up   103
Batting Averages Hit Bottom—Only One .300 Hitter in
A.L.   104
Senators, with Walter Johnson, Big Losers but Not the
Worst   104
Strange Demise of the Mets . . . A Little Bird Did Them
In   105


8. RECORD GAMES
Grimes Remembers Game When He Made 8 Outs in 4
At-Bats   107
In Heaviest Scoring Game, 26-23, Cubs Almost Blow 26-9
Lead in 7th!   111
Blue Jays Set New Record, Hammer 10 Homers in One
Game   114
Shortest Game in Pro Ball—9 Innings in 32 Minutes!   115
Minor League Records Surpass Majors—Except One for
Triples in a Season   116


9. OFF THE FIELD
Baseball Hall of Fame Houses Strange Specimens of the
Game   117
Drysdale Almost Failed to Make it to His Hall of Fame
Induction   120
Strange Scheduling: Oakland Plays Two Games in Two Cities
on One Day   122
Super Fan Missed Only One World Series Game in 42
Years   122
Babe's Signature Worth $500 But Beware! Some Are
Phony   124

ROSTER   125

# INTRODUCTION

## BASEBALL, A STRANGE CAREER

In many ways baseball is one of the strangest of all careers since a player has so short a period of time in which to earn his own particular niche in the game.

Many potential professional ballplayers start learning the basic skills—running, throwing, hitting, fielding—when they're still of Little League age, in the primary grades at school. An early start and a fierce dedication to the game are absolutely essential. Let's say, roughly speaking, that a young man begins his pro career at the age of 18. Almost certainly he will be forced to retire 20 years later, at 38 or so. By that time he's lost his fleetness afoot, speed of reflexes, and, perhaps, sharpness of eyes, among other things. At this age men in most other professions are just beginning to hit their stride.

Actually, a 20-year pro career is exceptional—the average length of a major league career is only 5 years. Players who can perform effectively into their late thirties and early forties (a group including Pete Rose, Darrell Evans, Tony Perez, Carl Yastrzemski, Phil and Joe Niekro, Tommy John, Hoyt Wilhelm and Nolan Ryan) are the exception rather than the rule.

Frankie Frisch, the old Hall of Fame second baseman, may have said it best: "When you get to the point where you really know what you're supposed to do on the ball field, you're just too damned old to be able to execute."

A legion of players have experienced serious withdrawal symptoms and faced severe psychological problems when they were forced to retire because of age. Included in this group are such great stars as Ty Cobb, Babe Ruth, Joe DiMaggio, Jimmie Foxx and Willie Mays.

"When you're forced to quit after playing for 20 and

more years, it's like going cold turkey," Jimmie Foxx once said. It's like withdrawing from any long-time obsession.

In closing his 22-year big league career with the New York Mets in 1973, Willie Mays grumbled to a reporter: "It's really tough to be 42, hitting .210 and sitting on the bench half the time."

This book, filled with true stories of strange moments and events, strange plays and players, batters and pitchers, and strange managers and owners, shows how they all fit into this strange game that forces players to try to compress their careers to "make it young," for only a few can even make it, much less make it a long career.

—Robert Obojski

# 1. STRANGE EVENTS

## ON MOTHER'S DAY, FELLER'S MOTHER STRUCK BY A FOUL BALL

It was a warm Mother's Day, May 14, 1939, almost cloudless throughout much of the Midwest, and an ideal day for baseball. Bob Feller, the 20-year-old fireballing phenom for the Cleveland Indians, was scheduled to face the Chicago White Sox at Comiskey Park—and for the occasion Feller's family, including his father, mother and 8-year-old sister, Marguerite, decided to drive from the homestead in Van Meter, Iowa, to Chicago, a distance of some 250 miles, to see the game.

The Fellers found themselves comfortably ensconced in grandstand seats between home and first base just before game time, and they watched as the Indians scored 2 runs in the first inning and 4 more in the third to take a 6-0 lead. Rapid Robert Feller was in rare form as he blanked the White Sox for the first two innings, not allowing a hit.

In the bottom of the third, Chicago third baseman Marvin Owen, a pinch hitter, had trouble getting around on Feller's 99-mile-an-hour fastball as he sent three straight soft fouls into the stands between first and home. On the next pitch, Owen swung late again, but this time he got the barrel of the bat on the ball and sent a vicious foul liner to the first base stands again—and to the exact spot where the Feller party was seated. There was no time to duck, and, tragically, the ball struck Mrs. Feller in the face.

As Feller followed through with his pitching motion, he could see clearly that his mother was struck by the ball. In recalling the incident years later, Feller said, "I felt sick, but I saw that Mother was conscious . . . I saw the police and ushers leading her out and I had to put down the impulse to run to the stands. Instead, I kept on pitching. I felt giddy and I became wild and couldn't seem to find

"Mama, watch out!"

the plate. I know the Sox scored three runs, but I'm not sure how.

"They immediately told me the injury was painful but not serious. There wasn't anything I could do, so I went on and finished the game and won. Then I hurried to the hospital.

"Mother looked up from the hospital bed, her face bruised and both eyes blacked, and she was still able to smile reassuringly.

"'My head aches, Robert,' she said, 'but I'm all right. Now don't go blaming yourself . . . it wasn't your fault.'"

14

Mrs. Feller spent a couple of days in the hospital and was released feeling no ill effects.

The Indians won that Mother's Day game 9-4 as Feller ran his record to 6-1. For the entire season he went 24-9 and struck out a major league-leading 246 batters.

In his autobiography *Strikeout Story* (New York: A. S. Barnes & Co., 1947), Feller emphasized that his mother was always a good soldier who helped to advance his baseball career in a thousand different ways.

Feller also said later: "It was a one in a million shot that my own mother while sitting within a crowd of people at a ball park would be struck by a foul ball resulting from a pitch I made." And on Mother's Day!

# STRANGE PINCH HITTER DRAWS ROARS WITH OUTRAGEOUS STUNT

It was Sunday, August 19, 1951, at Sportsman's Park, St. Louis, as the last place Browns tangled with the Detroit Tigers, who were also deep in the second division. The game was meaningless as far as standings were concerned.

During the season Bill Veeck, flamboyant owner of the Browns, had become a bit desperate because his rag-tag team floundered badly at the gate. (Total paid admissions for the year came to a sorry 294,000.)

As the late summer game progressed before the usual sparse Sportsman's Park crowd, Browns' manager Zack Taylor sent in a pinch hitter named Eddie Gaedel, who had never appeared in a professional game before. Tigers righthander Bob Cain walked Gaedel on four straight pitches, and after Eddie trotted down to first he was replaced by pinch runner Jim Delsing.

By this time the crowd was in an uproar. Pinch hitters had walked before, but none of them were as small as Gaedel, who stood 3 feet 7 inches tall and weighed 65 pounds, the normal size for a genuine midget. As Gaedel, wearing the number 1/8 on the back of his uniform shirt, swung his 17-inch bat menacingly at Pitcher Cain, he hollered, "Throw the ball right in here and I'll moider it!"

"I'll kill him if he swings the bat."

He had been told what to do. Bill Veeck wrote in his autobiography, "I spent many hours teaching him to stand straight up, hold his little bat high and keep his feet sprawled in a fair approximation of Joe DiMaggio's classic style. I told him I'll kill him if he swings the bat."

Plate umpire Ed Hurley had questioned Gaedel's credentials as a player, but under Veeck's able direction the midget had produced a standard major league contract from his hip pocket.

Bill Veeck, the "Barnum of Baseball," in all his years in the game had never gone this far before and succeeded in pulling off the greatest single outrageous stunt in the history of the game.

On the next day American League President Will Harridge turned thumbs down on any future Tom Thumbs by outlawing any further such travesty of the game.

Bill Veeck may have gained an enormous amount of notoriety for sending a midget to the plate, but nothing he did could save his franchise. After the 1953 season he was forced to sell the Browns, who in 1954 were transformed into the Baltimore Orioles.

As for Eddie Gaedel, his place in the standard baseball record books is secure. He compiled a perfect record as a pinch hitter, getting on base in his only time at bat.

## DON'T ROLL THAT TARPAULIN—COLEMAN MIGHT BE INSIDE!

Back in the old days, tarpaulins were spread out to cover baseball fields overnight and then rolled back manually by groundskeepers, but now electrically operated tarps have come into vogue. Push a button and it can be spread over the infield in a jiffy—push another button and it can be rolled back just as quickly.

One of the classiest of all powered retractable tarps is operated at St. Louis' Busch Stadium, and by sheer accident it became a cause célèbre during the 1985 League Championship Series played between the Cardinals and Los Angeles Dodgers. Vince Coleman, the Cards' star outfielder and base stealing king, happened to be standing on the tarp along the first base side, casually warming up before the series fifth game, when a ground-crew member, not realizing anyone was still on the tarp, activated the roll-up button. Within a second or two Coleman found himself trapped inside, being swallowed up as if a giant boa constrictor had wrapped its coils around him.

Coleman's screams brought out a rescue team, but not before some damage was done. His legs were so badly bruised that he could neither play in that fifth game, nor in the ensuing World Series that saw the Cardinals matched against the Kansas City Royals.

"The Coleman-tarpaulin episode certainly ranks as one of the strangest on-field accidents in baseball history," a St. Louis sportswriter commented.

"That tarp was a real man-eater," Coleman himself commented.

Sometimes when Busch Stadium is very quiet, one seems to hear faint murmurings from deep inside the tarpaulin machine, below the green artificial turf near first base.

"Vince," the machine seems to gurgle, like the crocodile seeking the rest of Captain Hook in *Peter Pan*. "Vince, come a little closer to me, Vince."

Coleman, sensing that the tarp machine's appetite is not yet satiated after it tried to ingest him, runs faster than ever now—away from that "monster" machine.

# TEBBETTS CROWNED BY BASKET OF TOMATOES IN "VEGETABLE WAR"

Throughout the tumultuous 1940 American League season, the Cleveland Indians, Detroit Tigers and New York Yankees were involved in a three-way dogfight for the pennant. The Yankees eliminated themselves in the campaign's final week by dropping a crucial game to the last place Philadelphia Athletics, while the Tigers, holding a two-game lead over the Indians, rode into Cleveland to play the final three games of the season.

Cleveland needed to win all three games, of course, in order to capture the flag.

Tensions always ran high between Detroit and Cleveland . . . for starters, the two teams formed a natural rivalry because of their geographical proximity, and over the run of the 1940 season a number of incidents exacerbated those tensions.

One of the worst of those incidents occurred on a late Thursday afternoon, September 19, before the final series. The Cleveland Indians rolled into Detroit's main railroad station just a few hours before a scheduled night game with the Tigers.

Somehow about a thousand Tiger fans discovered the hour when the Indians would be arriving at the station, and like a well-trained military unit they formed a gauntlet at the gate through which the players had to pass. The Tiger fanatics greeted the tribesmen with "Cry Babies, Cry Babies!" catcalls. (The Indians had been dubbed "Cry Babies" because in mid-season they had unsuccessfully

"Watch out below!"

mutinied against their autocratic manager, Oscar Vitt.) But worse than that, the Detroit fans heaved tomatoes, eggs, baby bottles and assorted other objects at the Indians. It was the beginning of the "Vegetable War."

When the Tigers were set to play the Indians in the season-closing series beginning on Friday afternoon, September 27, the stage was set for a titanic clash. In an unusual pitching match-up, Bob Feller, the Indians ace with a 27-10 record, squared off against Floyd Giebell, a virtually unknown 30-year-old rookie righthander, who had only pitched a handful of games in the majors. Tigers manager Del Baker threw Giebell into the game as a sacrificial lamb against Feller who was the odds-on favorite to capture his 28th victory. After all, Detroit needed only a single victory to take the pennant, and had to be stopped.

It was Ladies Day at Cleveland as some 20,000 screaming women jammed their way into Municipal Stadium with the total attendance very close to the 50,000 mark. In recalling that day years later, Bob Feller said:

"In that crowd were a great number of mysterious baskets and bags, carried by fans with revenge in their hearts. When Detroit's Hank Greenberg came up to take his swings in batting practice we got a sample of what was to come. A few tomatoes and eggs aimed at him came hurtling out of the upper deck. He grinned and waved at his tormentors.

"He didn't grin and wave in our half of the first inning, however. When Roy Weatherly, our centerfielder, lifted a high fly to left and he moved under it, the fans really cut loose with their ammunition. Greenberg was enveloped in a hail of vegetables, fruit and eggs as he wandered around under Weatherly's fly. I still wonder how he caught the ball instead of an orange.

"Leftfield looked as though a big produce train had been wrecked in it. Umpire Bill Summers angrily ripped off his mask and called time. Then, as the barrage continued, he went to the public address system and threatened to forfeit the game. Manager Vitt also spoke over the microphone, pleading for a chance to win the ball game. The threat and the plea stopped the throwing as park police circulated in the stands."

It took the Indians' grounds crew more than a half-hour to clear the debris from the field. Hank Greenberg, who had regained his composure, helped out, grabbing one of the wheelbarrows to cart off a pile of vegetables and fruits. "Hammerin' Hank" was always known for his sense of humor.

When play resumed, the big crowd had pretty much simmered down as the police continued to scout the stands for potential violators. Toward the end of the second inning, however, they cornered a suspect in the upper leftfield deck directly over the Tiger bullpen. As the police raced toward him the culprit dropped a heavy basket of tomatoes over the rail in order to rid himself of the evidence. Directly below, on a bullpen bench, unsuspecting catcher Birdie Tebbetts was hit squarely on the head by the basket and nearly knocked unconscious.

The police grabbed the perpetrator, a muscular 25-year-old factory worker named Carmen Guerra, and escorted him down to a lower deck security station. In the meantime, Tebbetts had recovered from the shock of the blow on the head and rushed to the area where the police were questioning Guerra. As the police held Guerra, an enraged Tebbetts allegedly punched the young man in the nose.

On the same day Guerra hired a lawyer and filed a $5,000 damage suit charging Tebbetts with assault and battery. Detroit club officials posted a $200 bond on the assault charge so that Tebbetts could leave town with the team. Later on, the suit was settled out of court.

In the fourth inning with the score 0-0, Feller walked Tiger second baseman Charlie Gehringer, and then Rudy York, the big first baseman, hit a curving lazy fly ball to leftfield just along the line. Ben Chapman raced over and seemed certain to make the catch, but the ball dropped into the stands just beyond his outstretched hands and only a few inches inside the foul line. This home run, that traveled little more than 320 feet, turned out to be the blow that finally did the Indians in.

Feller allowed no further runs after that point and was touched for a total of only three hits, but the obscure Floyd Giebell pitched with the ease of a seasoned performer and shut out the Indians, scattering six hits. Final score: Detroit 2, Cleveland 0.

The Tigers staged a raucous pennant-clinching party that afternoon, but the Indians won the next two games to finish exactly one game out of first place, and just a single game ahead of the third-place Yankees.

As for Floyd Giebell, he never won another game in the major leagues. He made the Tigers roster as a relief pitcher in 1941, but he lacked control and was belted around so much that he was soon sent back to the minors and never re-surfaced again into the majors.

That is strange baseball.

# TWO BALLS IN PLAY
# AT SAME TIME—AN
# UMPIRE'S MENTAL LAPSE

A college professor can be excused for being absentminded, but not a big league umpire during the course of a ball game. Because Vic Delmore became absentminded at a St. Louis Cardinals-Chicago Cubs game played at Wrigley Field on June 30, 1959, he caused one of the strangest and most bizarre plays in baseball history.

The Cards' top hitter Stan Musial was at bat with a 3-1 count when the next pitch got away from Cub catcher Sammy Taylor and skidded toward the backstop.

Umpire Delmore called "Ball four" and Musial trotted toward first. But Taylor and pitcher Bob Anderson argued vehemently with the ump that it was a foul tip.

Since the ball was still in play, and Taylor had not chased it, Musial ran toward second. Fast-thinking third baseman Alvin Dark then raced to the backstop and retrieved the ball. Meanwhile, Delmore was still involved in the argument with the Cub battery mates when he unthinkingly pulled a second ball out of his pocket and handed it to catcher Taylor. Suddenly noticing Musial dashing for second, pitcher Anderson grabbed the new ball and threw to second—at the same time that Dark threw to shortstop Ernie Banks with the original ball!

Anderson's throw sailed over second base into centerfield. Musial saw the ball fly past his head, so—not realizing there were two balls in play—he took off for third only to run smack into Banks who tagged him out with the original ball.

After a lengthy conference, the umpires ruled that Musial was out since he was tagged with the original ball.

Also called "out" was Vic Delmore himself. Citing a "lack of confidence" in Vic, National League President Warren Giles fired him at season's end.

# JACKIE ROBINSON GOT MINIMUM SALARY—$5,000 WHEN RICKEY BROUGHT HIM TO BIG LEAGUES

During the 1980s, baseball salaries reached a summit with utility infielders given contracts calling for $500,000 or more per season. A generation earlier, however, although the dollar bought more, salaries were generally so low that unionizing became inevitable.

Take the case of Lou Boudreau, star shortstop of the Cleveland Indians, who as a sophomore in 1940 played in every one of the team's 155 games, batted .295, drove in 101 runs, and led American League shortstops with a .968 fielding percentage. For that effort Boudreau played under a contract calling for the munificent sum of $5,000—which amounted to little more than $30 per game (or $60 for a doubleheader).

Indians' owner, Alva Bradley, a business tycoon with interests in myriad industries, felt guilty about that contract, so he gave Boudreau a $2,000 bonus at the season's close. Then Bradley doubled Boudreau's 1941 salary to $10,000. Of course, there were no television revenues at the time.

Jeff Heath, an Indians outfielder from 1936 to 1945, continuously complained about having to play for "peanuts." After he hit .343 and drove in 112 runs in 1938, he was given a contract for the 1939 campaign calling for about $3,000. When he finished his major league career with the Boston Braves in 1949, Heath signed a contract with the Pacific Coast League's Seattle Rainiers in 1950 worth $25,000, the highest baseball salary he ever received.

When Jackie Robinson, the first black in the Big Leagues, was promoted from the Montreal Royals of the International League in 1947 to the Brooklyn Dodgers under Branch Rickey, general manager, he gave Robinson a $5,000 contract, the major league minimum at the time.

# HIT A HOMER IN JAPAN
# AND WIN A SWORD

Earl Averill, Cleveland Indians hard-hitting centerfielder, was a part of the delegation of American League All-Stars who traveled to the Orient in the fall of 1934 to play a series of 16 exhibition games against a team consisting of Japan's top amateur and semi-professional players called the "All-Nippon Stars."

Averill's teammates included stars Babe Ruth and Lou Gehrig, sluggers Bing Miller, Charlie Gehringer and Jimmie Foxx, and pitchers Lefty Gomez and Earl Whitehill. The exhibitions were staged in cities throughout Japan, and by the time the series ended in late November the Americans had made a clean sweep by winning all 16 games.

One particular game between the Japanese and the Americans played at Itatsu Stadium in Kokura, an industrial city on the island of Kyushu, revealed quite graphically the almost limitless enthusiasm the Japanese have for baseball. Rain fell the night before the game, which was scheduled for 2 o'clock on November 26 and the precipitation continued steadily as game time approached. The fans, however, didn't allow bad weather to prevent them from seeing a contest they had been eagerly anticipating, particularly since this was the only appearance the two teams would make in Kokura.

Hard-core baseball aficionados began lining up at the gates outside the park at 5 A.M. and when the gates opened around noon some 11,000 persons had "bleacher" tickets. The catch was that there were no seats in the bleachers, which consisted only of the bare outfield turf. Unfortunately, the outfield was by then ankle deep in water and the hardy bleacherites had to stand, kneel, or squat in the shallow lake for the entire game. (The total crowd reached 20,000 that day since Itatsu Stadium had 9,000 permanent seats in addition to its "bleacher" capacity.) The fans in the outfield did not permit this minor inconvenience to dampen their enthusiasm for the big game, nor were they too disappointed when the All-Nippon Stars lost

24

"May I honor you with this sword?"

8-1. They saw a well-played contest and for the first time got a chance to view close up the big American stars, Babe Ruth and Lou Gehrig, about whom they'd read and heard so much.

One spectator, a middle-aged shopkeeper, walked 80 miles to see the game at Kokura, and he carried a sword which he vowed to give to the first American smashing a home run against the All-Nippon Stars. This valuable trophy was won by Earl Averill who drove a long homer into the rightfield seats. It was the highest possible honor he could have received: Among the Japanese, a sword was not only a weapon, but also the warrior's badge of honor—it was thought to be his very soul.

When we spoke with Averill at Cooperstown's Hotel Otesaga in July 1981, two years before his death, he recalled the 1934 Japanese tour and the game in Kokura: "That Japanese sword is the most unusual and prized trophy I ever received in baseball, and I've kept it in a glass case at my home in Snohomish [Washington] all these years."

Averill hit 8 home runs on the 1934 exhibition series, while Babe Ruth paced the long ball parade with 13 homers. The trip to Japan marked Babe Ruth's last appearance in a New York Yankees uniform, incidentally, since in February 1935 he was handed his unconditional release.

### Playing with Firecrackers

During his eleven-year tenure with the Cleveland Indians (1929–39), Earl Averill was a fun-loving, rollicking type of ballplayer who had the knack of keeping his teammates "loose" in the clubhouse and environs before a game. But one time he went too far with his merry ways and got himself into real trouble. While entertaining his fellow players with a mini-fireworks display in the home dugout at Cleveland's Municipal Stadium in 1935—around Fourth of July time—he miscalculated the power of a firecracker and almost blew his right hand off. He was taken to the hospital and remained out of action for two weeks.

What got a little "loose" was the dugout.

# IS BIG LEAGUE BASEBALL READY FOR LADY UMPIRES?

During the height of the Women's Liberation Movement in the early 1970s, Bernice Gera had a burning desire to fulfill her lifelong ambition of becoming a professional baseball umpire. In 1972 Bernice got her big chance when she was hired by the National Association of Professional Baseball Leagues to umpire in the Class A New York-Pennsylvania League. No other woman had ever umpired a professional game in the United States before.

In her first game as an arbiter Ms. Gera became involved in a hotly disputed call at home plate and when the last

"Excuse me, gentlemen."

out was made she resigned her post in disgust. Her umpiring career went up in smoke after just nine innings on the diamond.

Chris Wren became the second lady umpire to enter the professional ranks when in 1975 she was assigned by the National Association to work the Class A Midwest League. Chris proved to be a capable umpire and lasted three full years in the Midwest League, but left after the 1977 season to take a better paying job with the United Parcel Service.

Pam Postema, a native of Willard, Ohio, became a baseball aficionado while still in elementary school and in early 1977 at the age of 23 she entered the Al Somers Umpiring School, Daytona Beach, Florida. When the arduous three-month course was over, she finished 17th in her graduating class of 130.

The National Association took due note of Pam's budding talents as an umpire and assigned her to the Rookie Florida Gulf Coast League where she worked in 1977-78.

From that point Pam became the first lady ever to stick with umpiring on a career basis as she rose up the professional ladder. From the Gulf Coast League she was promoted to the Class A Florida State League where she called balls and strikes for two seasons. Her next two-year stop came with the Class AA Texas League, and from 1983 through 1986 she umpired in the Class AAA Pacific Coast League. In 1987 Pam switched to the Class AAA American Association where she remains. During the off-season she's kept herself sharp by working the Arizona Instructional and Caribbean Winter Leagues.

On July 27, 1987, Pam worked behind the plate at Cooperstown's annual Hall of Fame Game, this one matching the New York Yankees with the Atlanta Braves. She performed so efficiently that most of the 10,000 fans at Doubleday Field didn't even realize that a lady was behind the plate. Standing 5 feet 8 inches tall and weighing close to 150, and wearing her umpire's uniform, Pam Postema presents a clear-cut authority figure. Not once during the course of the game did any of the big leaguers seriously question any of her calls.

What does the future hold for Pam? The big leagues?

# GET THE X-RAY MACHINES READY! NO CORK IN THE BATS, PLEASE!

In a mid-August 1987 game against the San Francisco Giants, New York Mets third baseman Howard Johnson poled a mighty home run at Shea Stadium that allegedly measured about 480 feet. Roger Craig, Giants manager, charged out of the dugout and told the umpires the bat should be impounded and turned over to league officials for examination.

"There's no way Howard Johnson could hit a ball that far without the bat being corked," Craig fumed.

The Johnson bat was taken to National League President A. Bartlett Giamatti's office and from that point it was sent out to a nearby hospital where it was X-rayed for cork. The X-rays proved negative. No cork was found in the barrel.

"Check that one again."

According to newly established major league rules, the manager of each team is allowed to challenge one bat during the course of a game. Since challenges are being registered in so many games, both the National and American League offices are considering buying their own X-ray machines in order to cut down on fees being paid to hospitals!

When cork is placed in the barrel of a bat, the batter is able to speed up his swing and hit for greater distances. Bats are supposed to be constructed of wood and no other substance.

When Manager Craig registered his protest, he noted Howard Johnson never hit more than 12 homers in one season in his big league career through 1986 and he slammed more than 36 in 1987. He believed equipment tampering caused this phenomenon.

Ah, but Craig didn't realize that Johnson has been on well-planned weight and strength programs and has no need for corked bats in order to sock baseballs into orbit.

# "DEAD" BALLS, LOPSIDED BALLS—THEY WERE ALL PLAYABLE THEN

Nowadays the 26 major league teams use a total of some 400,000 baseballs during the course of the 162-game schedule, plus a couple of thousand more—at least—for the League Championships and World Series. If a ball shows the slightest scuff mark from hitting a wall, or if it picks up too much dirt from being hit to the ground, it's supposed to be thrown out of the game immediately.

So it's easy to see why 75 and more balls can be used in a single game. Remember, too, that lots of balls are fouled off into the stands.

However, back during the so-called "dead ball" days of the early 1900s, major league teams, along with the umpires, weren't nearly so free and easy in throwing bruised baseballs out of the game. Edd Roush, whom we interviewed before the 50th anniversary All-Star Game played at Chicago on July 6, 1983, had this to say about the quality of baseballs used in the big leagues:

"Before the lively ball came into use after 1920, the only way you could hit a homer was if the outfielder tripped and fell down. The 'dead ball' just wasn't wrapped tight, and lots of times I caught them out in centerfield when they were mashed on one side. Those lopsided balls still weren't thrown out of the game. Most of the time we'd use only four or five balls in a whole game."

Roush, whose big league career extended from 1913 to 1931, played mostly with the Cincinnati Reds and New York Giants. While with Cincinnati he won the National

"I wish the league could afford some new balls."

League batting crown in 1917 and 1919. Going into late 1987, Roush, at the age of 94, had the distinction of being the oldest living member of baseball's Hall of Fame.

"Let me get away from those fans."

# AUTOGRAPH HUNTERS ARE DANGEROUS TO A PLAYER'S HEALTH!

Running the gauntlet of autograph seekers can sometimes take its toll on a ballplayer. While many diamond stars try their best to accommodate fans, there are times when the clock says if you stop and sign, you'll pay a fine. In early August, 1987, New York Yankees outfielder Claudell Washington was running late for a night game in Kansas City. He tried valiantly to dodge the autograph seekers on his way into Royals Stadium and it cost him anyway. With a small army of clutching fans serving as an obstacle course, the trotting Washington tripped over someone's leg!

He was holding a briefcase in his left hand, and he tried using that hand to break the fall. The unhappy result was that Claudell scraped two fingers on his left hand so badly that he was unable to grip the bat properly and required more than a week on the bench before he could resume play.

The moral of this tale might be: If you're going to beat the autograph hounds, come to the park early or work on your end-around move.

## WILD THROWS CAN
## BE DANGEROUS

Sherry Robertson, Washington Senators infielder during the 1940s, was noted for his strong but erratic throwing. One time, early in his career, during infield practice he uncorked a mighty throw from shortstop. The ball went way over the first baseman's head and struck and *killed* a fan seated in the first-base boxes. The incident was not ruled an error, but an accident.

## HIT ON HEAD BY BAT
## WHILE IN ON-DECK CIRCLE

In 1945, Mobile catcher Harry Chozen had hit safely in 33 consecutive games and was on his way to setting a new Southern Association record of hitting safely in 49 consecutive games. Then, while kneeling in the on-deck circle, he was hit on the head and knocked unconscious by a flying bat that slipped out of the hands of teammate Pete Thomassie as he followed through on a vicious swing. Chozen was forced to retire from the game. After this episode, Chozen proceeded to hit safely in 16 additional games before being stopped. Southern Association President Billy Evans was called upon to rule and decided that Chozen's failure to get a hit in that July 6 game where he had walked in his only time at bat before being knocked out, did not break the hitting streak. The record Chozen broke had stood for 20 years.

Chozen's record is interesting in several other ways. Twice during the streak he was used as a pinch hitter and delivered. On two other occasions he entered the game in late innings, batting only once in each game, but he still managed to get his base hit. He broke the previous record of 46 in a truly dramatic manner by smashing a long home run in his first time at bat in his forty-seventh game. (Chozen's only big league experience came in 1937 at the age of 22, when he caught one game for the Cincinnati Reds. He had a single in four trips to the plate.)

In an August 1978 game, Los Angeles Dodgers catcher Steve Yeager wasn't quite as lucky as Harry Chozen in a batting circle accident. A Dodgers hitter broke his bat on a pitch causing a jagged piece of ash to sail straight for Yeager's throat. The team's trainer and doctor worked with lightning speed to remove the splintered wood from the jugular vein area. Yeager might otherwise have choked and bled to death. After a couple of weeks on the disabled list, Steve was back in action.

# "STONE AGE" GAVE FANS PLENTY OF EXCITEMENT

Sparkling fielding excites the crowd, and consistent field play results in great fielding averages.

Larry Bowa, National League shortstop for 16 years (1970–85), mostly with the Philadelphia Phillies and the Chicago Cubs, and currently the manager of the San Diego Padres, set many National League fielding records. These include rolling up an amazing .991 fielding percentage for the Phillies in 1978, committing only six errors in 683 total chances. In 2,247 major league games, all but 25 as a shortstop (all the others were played at second base), Bowa made only 211 errors out of 10,198 total chances for a .980 percentage, another all-time shortstop fielding record.

Another recordholder was Rich Dauer, Baltimore Orioles second baseman for a decade (1976-85), who committed only 75 errors in 5,013 total chances for a record .985 lifetime fielding percentage. Along the way, in 1978, Dauer

34

set another record by going through 86 consecutive games and handling 425 chances without making a single blunder.

Noted as a glove man, Don Money, Milwaukee Brewers third baseman, committed only 5 errors in 472 total chances in 1974, good for a record .989 fielding percentage. In that same season, Money set another record by going through 86 straight games and handling 257 chances without a single miscue. In 16 big league seasons with the Philadelphia Phillies and the Brewers (1968–83), Money, playing almost always at third base, made only 150 errors out of 6,089 chances, good for a lofty .975 fielding percentage. High fielding percentages at the "hot corner" are hard to come by.

By contrast infielders of an earlier era made errors by the gross. For example, William "Bad Bill" Dahlen, National League shortstop with Chicago, Brooklyn, New York and Boston from 1890 to 1913, committed the astounding total of 1,063 errors out of 14,294 total chances, resulting in a lowly .926 percentage. With Chicago in 1895, Dahlen led all National League shortstops in errors with 84.

However, that's still not the one-season record for big league shortstops by a long shot, since Bill Shindle of Philadelphia in the Players League made exactly 115 errors in 1890. Nevertheless, no major league fielder at any position made more errors lifetime than did Dahlen. Incidentally, he wasn't called "Bad Bill" because of his fielding—he earned the nickname by being a dangerous clutch hitter.

Most errors at the keystone sack, 828, is the unenviable record set by Fred Pfeffer, National League second baseman with Troy, Chicago, New York and Louisville for 16 years from 1882 to 1897. And it took Pfeffer only 1,670 games to make that many boots—that's almost one error for every two games.

Hall-of-Famer John McGraw may well have established the record for the lowest lifetime fielding average at third base, .899. In a major league playing career that spanned 16 seasons, or parts of seasons, with Baltimore and New York from 1891 to 1906, "Mugsy" McGraw miscued 394 times in 3,917 total chances. We must hasten to add that McGraw played a few games at second base now and then, but at any infield position he was a real "butterfingers." Good that

McGraw earned his laurels as the Giants manager. We must also hasten to add that McGraw was not playing for also-rans—he was performing for championship teams.

Rattling off all these statistics does not necessarily mean that ballplayers of two and three generations ago were all that inferior as compared with today's denizens of the diamonds. Rather, the equipment used by the old-timers was clearly inferior, especially the fielders' gloves.

The old-time gloves, often dubbed "motormen's mitts," were small pieces of hard black leather that barely covered the hand. Many of them didn't even have fingers.

Today's gloves, on the other hand, are veritable miracles of the leather workers' art. The contemporary mitts are huge as compared with those used from the 1880s to the early part of the 20th century, and they come with enormous webs to enable fielders to snag balls that would have entirely eluded the old-timers.

"The 'crabnets' they use today make fielding almost fumble proof," observed Luke Appling who committed 672 errors while shortstopping for the Chicago White Sox from 1930 to 1950.

Moreover, groundskeeping has evolved almost as a fine art, with today's fields usually being kept in excellent shape. Some of the big league fields utilized during baseball's so-called "Stone Age" weren't kept much better than cow pastures, with bumps and hollows. Consequently, with a smooth field the ball has a much better chance of taking a "true bounce." And with artificial turf used in so many parks today, very few balls will take a bad bounce. They may bounce high unexpectedly but generally stay straight unless they hit a seam in the indoor carpet, as happened in the 1987 World Series.

Connie Mack, whose professional career as a player and manager stretched on for more than 65 years, from 1884 to 1950, once remarked that the error—the unexpected element in baseball—constitutes one of the most exciting plays in the game. "Take the error out of the game and baseball will be dead within a month," Mack stoutly maintained.

Well, judging by the bushels of errors committed in big league baseball 50 to 100 years ago, the game back then was certainly vibrantly alive and kicking.

# CENTERFIELDER CARLISLE
# MAKES UNASSISTED
# TRIPLE PLAY

The unassisted triple play is one of the rarest plays in baseball, with only 8 having occurred in the major leagues and only a handful in the minors.

But Walter Carlisle, a centerfielder for the Vernon team (in Los Angeles), on July 19, 1911, in a game against the Los Angeles Angels, executed perhaps the most spectacular unassisted triple play in professional baseball history.

With the score tied in the ninth inning, Charles Moore and George Metzger of the Angels walked. Pitcher Al Carson of Vernon was replaced by Harry Stewart. The Angels' third baseman, Roy Akin, connected on Stewart's first pitch for a low line drive over second base for what appeared to be a clean single. Moore from second and Metzger from first were off running on a hit-and-run signal. Carlisle, playing in close behind second, lunged forward and caught the liner just off the turf, ending with a somersault, landing on his feet (he had been a circus acrobat). He raced to second base and touched the bag, while Moore was well on his way to the plate; then he trotted to first, touching the bag to retire Metzger, who was still well past second.

Carlisle's name is secure in the record books since he is the only *outfielder* to have pulled off the unassisted triple play. (Tris Speaker, the Hall of Fame centerfielder active in the majors 1907–28, mostly with the Boston Red Sox and Cleveland, usually played in close and made several unassisted *double plays*, but never came close to running off the solo triple play.)

In recognition of Carlisle's singular achievement, the Vernon and Los Angeles fans presented him with a diamond-studded gold medal.

# THE DAY COBB AND SISLER
# WERE MOUND OPPONENTS

On October 4, 1925, fans saw the unusual spectacle of two managers, both renowned hitters, PITCH against each other in the season's finale. Righthander Ty Cobb of the Detroit Tigers hurled one perfect inning and lefthander George Sisler of the St. Louis Browns worked 2 scoreless innings in an 11-6 Tiger victory. Neither Cobb nor Sisler figured in the decision.

Cobb, who occasionally threw batting practice, had pitched 4 innings in a couple of games for the Tigers back in 1918—and that was extent of his mound experience.

Sisler, however, broke into the majors with the Browns in 1915 as a pitcher, and it was Branch Rickey, the Browns' manager at the time, who converted the "Sizzler" into a first baseman because of his ability as a hitter. Sisler was primarily a pitcher during his college days at the University of Michigan where he earned a degree in engineering. Interestingly, Sisler's baseball coach at Michigan was Branch Rickey, who also served as athletic director.

# CRAMER AND WILLIAMS:
# A CLASSIC COLLISION IN
# THE OUTFIELD

When this writer was still in the primary grades, he saw one of his first big league games ever at Cleveland's Municipal Stadium on Sunday, June 23, 1940, as the Indians faced the Boston Red Sox.

In the eighth inning, Cleveland second baseman Ray Mack lined a drive deep into the left centerfield gap, with centerfielder Doc Cramer and leftfielder Ted Williams converging on the ball. In their mad dash they didn't see each other, collided head-on, and were both knocked unconscious as the ball rolled to the gate at the 463-foot sign. Mack got an easy inside-the-park homer.

Cramer was the first to get up and after getting a whiff of smelling salts from the trainer he was able to continue on in the game, but poor Ted Williams was carried off the field on a stretcher and taken to a local hospital to have his fractured jaw repaired. "Ted the Kid" remained hospitalized for a couple of days and missed more than a week's worth of action.

It was always my impression that the collision was Cramer's fault because he was a 12-year big league veteran and should have directed the play on Mack's drive, while Williams was only a 22-year-old sophomore in the league at the time.

We finally got our chance to question Williams about the play 47 years after it happened, at the 1987 Hall of Fame Induction Ceremonies at Cooperstown. Williams said:

"Hell no, don't blame that collision on Cramer, it was my fault. I took off like crazy after Mack's liner and ran into Doc . . . if I left him alone, he would have had a good chance to flag it down. From that day on, I tried to look where I was going in the outfield."

## STRANGE GAME IN CUBA: GUNFIRE AROUND THE BALL PARK

Al Cicotte, who pitched for the New York Yankees, Cleveland Indians, St. Louis Cardinals and Houston Astros from 1957 to 1962, recalled playing in the Cuban Winter League during turbulent days just at the time when Fidel Castro had come to power after overthrowing Dictator Fulgencio Batista.

While he was pitching a game for Mariano against the Havana Sugar Kings at Havana Stadium on January 4, 1959, "there were tough-looking weatherbeaten soldiers from Castro's army all over the playing field, and two of them insisted on catching my warm-up pitches in the bullpen. The game started out quietly enough, but as I walked out to the mound to start the third inning, I heard a volley of rifle and machine-gun fire—approximately 12 to 15 shots in all—from about two blocks' distance in the general direction of the centerfield fence. While going through my motions on the pitching rubber, I immediately stopped everything I was doing as the entire crowd lapsed into a strange silence.

"We all waited for a few moments and, hearing no more shots, the umpire broke the silence by shouting 'Play Ball!' The game moved along without further incident into the sixth inning when I noticed groups of fans 'buzzing' everywhere in the stadium. The players in our dugout were told that several die-hard Batista army officers had had a running gunfight around third inning time with Castro's troops. The Batista officers were killed during the battle. After all this, our ball game didn't seem to be very important, although we were still battling for the Winter League pennant."

Cicotte, property of the Cleveland Indians at the time, left the Mariano team three weeks before the Winter League season ended. The Indians management insisted he come home because they didn't want one of their players to be exposed to stray hails of gunfire.

# 2. STRANGE PLAYERS

## PIERSALL CLUBS 100TH HOMER, RUNS THE BASES BACKWARDS

When Jimmy Piersall, one of the most uninhibited spirits in baseball history, slammed out his 100th major league homer while playing for the Washington Senators in 1963, he celebrated the occasion by running the bases *backwards* and sliding into home plate. Piersall probably thought at the time that this was going to be his last big home run—actually he managed to hit four more before he retired in 1967. Anyway, the league ruled that running the wrong way was illegal hereafter.

## FROM BIG LEAGUE BALLPLAYER TO EVANGELIST: "BILLY" SUNDAY

"Let's put it over the plate for Jesus!" roared William Ashley "Billy" Sunday as he wound up like a pitcher with an imaginary baseball in his right hand during one of the many thousands of exhortations he delivered as America's most renowned evangelist of the late 19th century.

Billy Sunday, born at Ames, Iowa, on November 19, 1862, spent part of his boyhood in orphanages since his father, a private in the Twenty-Third Infantry Volunteers, died during the Civil War. He never saw his father. The boy's difficult early life steeled him for a career that was to make him a legendary figure in American history.

As a teenager in Marshalltown, Iowa, Billy Sunday became intensely interested in baseball and gained quick distinction as a speedy outfielder on a crack local amateur team. In fact, his phenomenal base running had made him a local celebrity.

Adrian C. "Cap" Anson, the famed player-manager of the Chicago White Stockings and a native of Marshalltown, chanced to see young Billy in action and proceeded to sign him to a contract. So Billy Sunday jumped directly from the sandlots of Marshalltown to the major leagues. That was in 1883 when he was 20.

The jump was almost too big for Billy since he struck out in his first 13 trips to the plate for Chicago. However, Cap Anson took him under his wing and exercised great patience—and at season's end Billy wound up hitting a respectable .241, going 13 for 54.

Cap Anson became a father figure to Billy and exercised a positive influence over him. "Big Anse" was a fanatic about physical conditioning—in a day when most ballplayers ate and drank as heartily as they could afford to, Cap ate no fried foods, drank no strong drink, was a non-smoker and avoided potatoes and sweets. Billy Sunday followed Cap's example religiously. (Anson, incidentally, played in the major leagues until he was 45 and became the first player to amass more than 3,000 base hits.)

At 5 feet 10 inches and 160 pounds, Sunday batted left-handed and never became more than an average spray hitter, but he was always a demon on the base paths. In 1887, in his fifth and last season with Anson's White Stockings, he stole 34 bases in 50 games and was acknowledged as the champion sprinter of the National League. This led to a match with Arlie Latham, St. Louis infielder, who held similar honors in the rival American Association (then a major league). In the 100-yard race, which drew national attention, Sunday won by no less than 15 feet! (Latham was no pushover either, for in 1887 he pilfered 129 bases in 136 games.)

At first Sunday was reckless on the bases—almost a wild man—but Anson taught him how to steal and how to run bases intelligently. Sunday's speed and daring as both a base runner and outfielder made him one of the great crowd favorites in the National League of the 1880s.

In 1888 Sunday was traded to Pittsburgh (simply called the "Pittsburghs" at the time) where he turned in a solid

42

performance. His batting average came to a relatively low .236 in 120 games, but he stole 71 bases and scored 69 runs—pretty good offensive stats for those days. In the field he continued to scintillate as one of the best ballhawks in the majors.

Sunday continued as a terror on the bases in 1889, swiping 47 sacks in 81 games and scoring 62 runs while inching up his batting average to .240. He went from Pittsburgh to Philadelphia in a late season trade in 1890 and was a major asset to both clubs, stealing 84 bases and scoring 84 runs while hitting a respectable .258 in 117 games.

Billy Sunday is now ranked as one of the really bright lights of the National League, but in the spring of 1891, at 28, he decided to chuck his rising baseball career and enter the Y.M.C.A.—and evangelical work. Baseball fans around the country were dismayed at hearing the news.

Leaving baseball was a very tough decision for Sunday. He was still two years short of 30, still developing, and just approaching the peak of his career on the diamond.

In his eight years in the big leagues, Sunday batted a modest .248 in 499 games (with 498 hits for 2,007 at-bats), but his race-horse running on the base paths and in the outfield made him a real standout. Unfortunately, stolen base records were not kept for the first four years of his career, but statisticians have calculated that he stole more than 300—a remarkable achievement. Though he wound up like a pitcher on the public-speaking platform, he hurled in only a single game in the majors as a reliever for part of an inning with Philadelphia in 1890.

He had been converted in 1887 at a Chicago mission, and from that time on his interest in religion steadily deepened. Though he had a three-year contract with Philadelphia, he obtained a release from the team's owners by explaining that he had "a call from God" to enter evangelical work.

The Philadelphia owners had pleaded with Sunday to change his mind and fulfill the terms of his contract. They naturally thought his attitude was very strange indeed since he was walking away from baseball just as he was on the verge of becoming one of the top-paid players in the game.

In answer to those entreaties, Sunday kept repeating that he needed to respond to a "higher calling."

Just before the beginning of the 1891 season, the Cincinnati Reds, recognizing that Billy Sunday was a free agent, offered him a contract calling for $3,500—that came out to $500 per month for a seven-month season, excellent money in those days. Sunday turned it down flat to accept a position in the Chicago Y.M.C.A. as a "subordinate secretary" at $83.33 per month, and, as Billy recalled, "Sometimes this was six months overdue."

Here Billy Sunday came under the influence of Dwight L. Moody (1837–99), a past president of the Chicago "Y," who unquestionably ranks as the great American evangelist of the latter half of the 19th century. Moody conducted his evangelistic campaigns throughout the U.S.A., Canada, Mexico and Great Britain, and in the process he led hundreds of thousands of persons to accept and confess Christ as Savior. Billy Sunday wanted to emulate Dwight L. Moody.

Billy remained with the Chicago "Y" through 1895, becoming assistant secretary, and then in 1896 he began his evangelical work in earnest. In 1903 he was ordained into the Presbyterian ministry, earning a Doctor of Divinity degree along the way. Almost until the time of his death on November 6, 1935, just a few days shy of his 73rd birthday, Billy Sunday preached the gospel constantly. The number of persons converted under his preaching is estimated at more than 300,000.

## Billy Sunday Batted Best Against Booze

Billy Sunday's main theme centered around "Battling with Booze." He deeply believed that hard liquor was the bane of all mankind, and if it were to be eliminated completely we'd all be well on the road to Utopia. Sunday traveled incessantly, especially throughout the Midwest and Eastern U.S. He toured many states, including Iowa, Illinois, Pennsylvania and West Virginia in special trains, campaigning for temperance. During one of his campaigns in Johnstown,

Billy Sunday railed against booze and tobacco.

Pennsylvania, 10,000 men in one meeting organized themselves into a "Billy Sunday Anti-Saloon League."

In Iowa, literally scores of towns and counties were reported as having "gone dry" as a direct result of the Billy Sunday meetings. Some 13 or 15 towns in Illinois visited by Sunday in a two-week period voted out the saloon.

In a typical temperance speech filled with fire Billy Sunday would exhort: "The saloon is the sum of all villainies. It is worse than war or pestilence. It is the crime of crimes. It is the parent of crimes and the mother of sins. It is an appalling source of misery and crime in the land. And to license such an incarnate fiend of hell is the dirtiest, low-down, damnable business on top of this old earth. There is nothing to be compared with it."

And then Sunday hit at the nation's breweries by quoting from "De Brewer's Big Hosses," an 1880s temperance poem reading in part:

"Oh, de Brewer's big hosses, comin' down de road,
Totin' all around ole Lucifer's load;
Dey step so high, an' dey step so free,
But dem big hosses can't run over me . . ."

Through his fervent campaign against intoxicants of all types Billy Sunday became a major influence in the adoption of the Eighteenth Amendment to the Constitution which prohibited the manufacture and sale of all liquors in the United States. The Prohibition Amendment went into force in 1920, and was not repealed until 1933. The "Noble Experiment" had failed. (Billy Sunday wouldn't appreciate TV baseball sponsorship by the breweries.)

Social historian Harvey Wish observed: "Both Dwight L. Moody and Billy Sunday ignored the basic economics and social abuses of the day except for their heated campaigns against the saloon. To the fundamentalist, Sabbath-breaking and drink were the chief social problems of the times."

There is no question, nonetheless, that Billy Sunday made a major impact upon American history.

## Sunday Disdained Tobacco, Too, But Was Pictured on Cigarette Cards

It should also be emphasized that Sunday strongly disliked tobacco in any form, whether used for smoking, chewing or sniffing. While with the White Stockings, he continuously chastised his teammate, pitcher John Clarkson, for excessive smoking. Once when Sunday spotted Clarkson coming out of a hotel room bathtub, he observed: "Clarkson had so much nicotine on his body from handling cigarettes that the bathtub water turned brown."

Clarkson did make it to the Hall of Fame with a 327-176 record, but he died at the age of 47 from lung cancer.

Lew Lipset, baseball memorabilia dealer from Centereach, New York, commented in a recent edition of his bi-monthly newsletter, The Old Judge: "It seems every year or two there's one old player who develops a near-cult following. In the mid-1980s it was Joe Jackson. Now it appears to be Billy Sunday. Anyone having vintage tobacco cards portraying Billy Sunday should know that they're commanding record prices today."

46

From 1886 to 1890, Sunday was portrayed on a variety of collectors' cards inserted into packs of "Old Judge" and other brands of cigarettes. One may wonder why Billy Sunday allowed his photograph to be imprinted on cards issued by cigarette companies since he was so clearly opposed to the use of tobacco in any form. But in the 1880s, individual players didn't have too much to say about where their photos appeared.

Lipset believes that in many cases the cigarette manufacturers approached the team owners for permission and got it without the players' consent.

# THE STRANGE CASE OF ALAN "INKY" STRANGE

No book entitled "Baseball's Strangest Moments" would be complete without a mention of Alan "Inky" Strange, American League shortstop of the 1930s and early 1940s. He was a brilliant fielder wherever he played and a strong minor league hitter who could never quite solve major league pitching.

Strange came up with the St. Louis Browns in 1934 at the age of 24, played 127 games, and hit a weak .233 when higher averages were in vogue. He started the 1935 campaign with the Browns, found himself traded to Washington in midseason, and then spent the next four years in the minors.

He had his "career year" in pro ball in 1939 with Seattle of the Pacific Coast League when he clubbed a circuit-leading 55 doubles while performing with his usual aplomb in the field.

That earned him a promotion back to the St. Louis Browns in 1940 where he remained through 1942, being used primarily as a utility infielder. After that, Strange never again resurfaced in the majors. In a total of 314 American League games, he hit .223.

Why couldn't a player of Strange's considerable ability ever quite make it in the big leagues? It seems that he couldn't hit a good curve ball. Once pitchers discover a player is primarily a fastball hitter, they feed him a steady diet of curves. That's what happened to Strange.

Baseball historian Bill Borst, who has written several books and numerous articles on the St. Louis Browns, observed recently: "Alan Strange typified the average Brownie . . . he had a great deal of promise but that promise was never really fulfilled."

# THE STRANGE CASE
# OF PETE GRAY,
# ONE-ARMED OUTFIELDER

Good ballplayers were extremely scarce during World War II, and the public, as well as the government, wanted baseball to carry on. The result was that many of the big leaguers of the 1942–45 period were those who were too young for the draft, or were classified 4-F (not physically fit for military duty).

The most famous 4-F of them all was one-armed outfielder Pete Gray, who had batted a solid .333 and had stolen 68 bases for the Memphis Chicks in 1944, achievements that won him election as the Southern Association's Most Valuable Player. Gray became the talk of the big league world because his play in the S.A. was so impressive. The lowliest team, the St. Louis Browns, eagerly signed him for the 1945 campaign.

Gray had lost his right arm at the bicep in a boyhood accident, but he developed his left arm to such a degree and compensated for his handicap with such quickness that he became a really solid ballplayer. Gray had started out as a sandlot player in the Nanticoke, Pennsylvania, area as a teenager, and landed his first professional contract with Three Rivers, Ontario, of the Canadian-American League in 1942 at the age of 25. From that point he moved up the minor league ladder rapidly.

This writer saw Gray in action several times with the Browns in 1945 and recalls vividly his performance against the Indians at Cleveland's Municipal Stadium in one particular four-game series in early June. Gray cracked out 7 hits, including a triple and a double—both hard-hit line

Pete Gray, wartime phenomenon.

drives to deep leftcenter—in 17 at-bats. Moreover, he fielded his leftfield post flawlessly. After catching a fly ball,
he would flip his glove under the stump of his right arm
in a rapid-fire motion so that he could throw the ball with
his bare left hand.

Gray batted only .218 in the tough American League
competition. Amazingly enough, however, he struck out
only 11 times in 234 official at-bats. When Gray took the
field either in a minor league or major league park, no
one ever did him any favors—he got along on his own
grit. As a result, he became an inspiration during and after
the war to the multitude of disabled U.S. war veterans.

Gray unfortunately found himself back in the minors
once the war was over. He retired from active play after
a season with Dallas of the Texas League in 1949.

# "GOOFY" GOMEZ STOPS PITCHING IN WORLD SERIES TO WATCH PASSING AIRPLANE

Vernon "Lefty" Gomez, one of the most colorful players in big league history, anchored the New York Yankees pitching staff during the 1930s as he became a 20-game winner four times and wound up with an imposing 189-102 career record. Moreover, he won six World Series games without a loss (a record) and went 3-1 in 1930s All-Star competition. He was elected to the Hall of Fame in 1972.

No matter how critical the situation became on the baseball field, Lefty never lost his sharp sense of humor, and because of his constant practical joking he became known as "El Goofo" or just plain "Goofy" Gomez.

Gomez' most memorable goof occurred during the second game of the 1936 World Series against the hard-hitting New York Giants at the Polo Grounds.

More than 50 years after this episode Gomez remembered it well as he related:

"It was early in the game, I was a little wild and before I knew it there were two runners on base. Suddenly I heard a plane flying over the ball park—it was a big airliner—and I just stepped off the mound, forgot about the runners, the batter, the game and everything else. I stood there watching calmly, until the plane completely disappeared from sight.

"Sure, I kept 45,000 fans (as well as the players) waiting and everyone wondered why I stopped the game this way . . . some people thought I was just plain crazy. Well, I was a little tense and I wanted to ease the tension a bit. As I recall, I came out of that inning pretty well unscathed."

The Yankees went on to whip the Giants 18-4 as Gomez went the distance, walking 7 and striking out 8.

The mists of antiquity may have settled a bit on the details of that game, but Lefty Gomez will always be remembered as the player who stopped the World Series dead in its tracks to watch an airplane in flight.

After Lefty Gomez finished recalling the 1936 World Series he went on to reminisce:

"Certainly one of my greatest moments in baseball came in the spring of 1930 when I first got into the big leagues with the New York Yankees and became a teammate of Babe Ruth. Ruth was the greatest single character I ever came in contact with. On the ball field he was a genius . . . there wasn't anything he couldn't do.

"One time, in about the summer of 1932, he was out at an all-night formal party and came into the Yankees clubhouse in his tuxedo, without having so much as a wink of sleep. As soon as he began putting on his uniform his eyes began to clear up, and that afternoon he led the Yankees to a victory over the White Sox by smashing a couple of homers."

# YOGI BERRA STRIKES OUT THREE TIMES, "NOT NOWHERE" WILL HE PLAY LIKE THAT

Yogi Berra is one of the power hitters of yesteryear who almost always seemed to get his bat on the ball, and managed to keep his strikeouts down to an extremely low level.

When he came up with the Yankees at the tail end of the 1946 season, Berra indicated quite clearly through his performance in the seven games he got in that he wasn't going to let too many third strikes slip by him. In those seven games he bashed 2 homers and struck out only once. From that point on, Berra, a lefthanded pull hitter who was built like a fireplug (he stood 5 feet 8 inches high and weighed a solid 190 pounds), enjoyed five full seasons where his homers exceeded his K's: 1950—28, 12; 1951—27, 20; 1952—30, 24; 1955—27, 20; and 1956—30, 29.

In nearly two decades of big league play (1946–65), covering 2,120 games, Yogi hit 358 homers against only 415 strikeouts Moreover, in 14 World Series from 1947 to 1963, covering 75 games, Berra hammered 12 homers against only 17 strikeouts.

Berra didn't play at all in 1964 when he managed the pennant-winning Yankees, and, after he was fired for losing the World Series, he landed on his feet as a coach for the New York Mets in 1965.

The struggling Mets needed an extra catcher badly, and so, Berra, then 40, was pressed into service. Berra saw action in only four games before he threw in the towel. In one of the games he struck out three times and told reporters afterward: "I never struck out three times in one game before: not in the big leagues, not in the minor leagues, not in the little leagues, not nowhere. Now it's time to quit for good."

If everyone in the big leagues today who struck out three times in one game would voluntarily retire himself, the playing ranks would be almost decimated.

# ROSE'S STRANGE RETIREMENT FROM ACTIVE PLAY

"In all the years I've been in baseball, I've never seen anyone more statistics conscious than Pete Rose," Johnny Bench once said of his teammate on Cincinnati's "Big Red Machine" of the 1970s. "Pete keeps close track of everything: hits, batting average, runs scored, RBIs, the works . . . we should have more like him," Bench concluded.

And after 24 years in the big leagues, Rose managed to roll up a series of enormous stats that stand as all-time records, including: games played: 3,562; times at bat: 14,053; and base hits: 4,256. His 2,165 runs scored ranks near the top on the all-time list.

Rose seemed driven to add to his records, but strangely after August 17, 1986 he never put himself back into the lineup though he was by now player-manager of the Cincinnati Reds. In the last three games he played in, he went 8 for 15 and in one game in that short stretch he blazed like a meteor, going 5 for 5. With that hot streak, Rose brought his batting mark up to .218 for the season (it had been a bit under .200) and he seemed to have regained his old stroke. At that point he sat himself down for the rest of the season, but he never announced his retirement from active play.

Everyone expected Rose to play at least on a part-time basis in 1987 and in midseason when the Reds' attack was floundering he began taking serious batting practice as he prepared to insert himself into the lineup. He never did. Though he was 46, he seemed in excellent shape.

Toward the end of the season Marge Schott, Reds owner, asked Pete to play in a couple of farewell games. He didn't heed the request and remained strictly a bench manager for the entire year. Reporters continuously asked Rose if he planned to play again, but the answers were always noncommittal.

Everyone expected that long awaited, pre-announced farewell appearance from Pete Rose, but it never came. Strange, strange, strange.

# STRANGE BATTING STYLE LEADS OH TO HOME RUN HITTING RECORD

Sadaharu Oh, the famous (in Japan) Tokyo Giants lefthanded-hitting first baseman, early in his career adopted an unusual batting style. He kicked up his right leg in flamingo style and then planted his left foot on the ground at the moment of contact of bat and ball. Some of his critics said he looked like "a one-legged swinging scarecrow," but in a 22-year career that stretched from 1959 to 1980 Mr. Oh managed to belt 868 regular season homers, far and away a world professional record.

Hank Aaron, the U.S. major league home run champion hit "only" 755 homers. The Japanese insist that their two six-team professional leagues, the Central and the Pacific, are true major leagues. (The Tokyo Giants play in the Central League.)

Most American baseball experts agree that Oh could have easily succeeded in the U.S. big leagues, though he wouldn't have hit as many homers, since the Japanese ball parks are a bit smaller than those in the States.

Oh, born on May 20, 1940 in Tokyo, the son of a Japanese mother and a Chinese father, stood 5 feet 10 inches and weighed 180 pounds in his playing days. Though he never broke Roger Maris' single season record of 61 homers in a 162-game season, he did reach 55 in his best season in 1964 in the Japanese league regular season of only 140 games.

Called "The Japanese Babe Ruth," Oh was appointed as Tokyo Giants manager, after his retirement from active play.

# CATCHERS ARE A STRANGE BREED: LOPEZ, BOONE AND BATEMAN PRIME EXAMPLES

When a player dons the "tools of ignorance" and takes a stand behind the plate, he knows he's taking a risk of getting his fingers broken and his legs and feet bruised, not once but many times.

Al Lopez was brave enough to set the world record of 1,918 games behind the plate in his 20 years in baseball, 1928-47.

Interestingly, when Al Lopez was managing the Indians in the 1950s, one of his star players, 1951 to 1953, was a hard-hitting shortstop-third baseman named Ray Boone. Papa Boone used to bring his little son, Bob, always dressed up in a baseball uniform to the game and let him work out on the sidelines.

Lopez may have given the younger Boone some tips on catching at the time or just set a fine example, but little did he know that this tot would eventually break Lopez' own endurance record for catchers.

That's exactly what Bob did.

Bob Boone (born November 19, 1947) accomplished the feat in a relatively short time period, fewer than 15 full major league seasons. After spending nearly five years in the minor leagues, he broke in with the Philadelphia Phillies in the latter part of the 1972 campaign, became their regular catcher the next year, and 9 years later was traded to the Angels at the beginning of 1982.

Along the way he also played a few games in the outfield and at third and first base, but those don't count toward the record, of course.

At the conclusion of his record-breaking game, Boone, the new "King of Squat," commented: "The record means I've taken more aspirin and other forms of pain-killers than any other player in history." Then he added the obligatory "I play baseball to help my team win, not for personal goals or records."

The Hall of Fame in Cooperstown requested Boone's glove for display, but the rugged backstop's reply was "No, I've still got some games to catch with it."

Another catcher, John Bateman, a hulking 6-foot-3-inch 225-pounder, hit 81 home runs in a 10-year big league career with the Houston Astros, Montreal Expos and Philadelphia Phillies from 1963 to 1972, and wound up as a softball star. A righthanded hitter with pretty fair power, Bateman required 1,017 games in baseball to knock out those 81 homers.

After Bateman was released by the Phillies early in 1973, he had to be content to play with the Houston Bombers softball team for the next several years. One day toward the end of 1976 Eddie Feigner saw Bateman smash a mammoth 450-ft softball homer at the Houston Astrodome.

Feigner went to Bateman and promptly signed him up for his "The King and His Court," a four-man softball team. Feigner was such a great softball pitcher that he required only three "back-up" men on his team (a shortstop, first baseman and catcher) to contend on even terms against a regular 10-player softball team.

Bateman fit in well with Feigner and his "Court," and in his first full season in top level fast-pitch softball in 1978 he connected for 179 homers in 221 games. In one game, he hit five. At season's end Bateman chortled: "Who needs the big leagues? With "The King and His Court" I hit for a better average, drive out more homers, and play on a winner. In fact, I make better money playing softball than I did hardball."

55

## BOBO NEWSOM
## DISDAINS PERFUME

Louis Norman "Bobo" Newsom, who pitched for eight major league and eight minor league teams from 1929 to 1953, was considered one of the roughest, toughest competitors ever to step on the pitcher's mound. At the height of his career with the pennant-winning Detroit Tigers in 1940, he was asked by a fragrance company to endorse a perfume.

Newsom, who was never averse to making an extra dollar, turned the offer down flat when he said: "Any fee I would receive wouldn't be worth the heckling I'd get from opposition dugouts."

# 3. STRANGE EXECUTIVES

## OWNER STEINBRENNER, BASEBALL'S DR. JEKYLL AND MR. HYDE

In 1886, Robert Louis Stevenson published one of his best known stories, *The Strange Case of Dr. Jekyll and Mr. Hyde.* In this horror-fantasy, Stevenson spins a tale of a man with a dual personality: Dr. Jekyll, the brilliant physician, is able to periodically transform himself into the viciously criminal Mr. Hyde. Of all the major figures in baseball today, George M. Steinbrenner III stands as, perhaps, the most controversial because of his obvious dual personality.

On the one hand, Steinbrenner is able to perform extremely magnanimous deeds, and on the other he does many perfectly awful things, though in no way do we suggest that he gets nearly as nasty as Mr. Hyde.

Before Steinbrenner became principal owner of the New York Yankees in 1973, he owned the Cleveland Pipers professional basketball team which nearly went bankrupt, and from that point he was anxious to gain control of a major sports franchise so that he could turn it into a success. His fortune is based on his ownership of the American Shipbuilding Co., now based in Tampa, Florida. Here we'll offer a brief representative list of five "Mr. Hydes" for Steinbrenner and five "Dr. Jekylls."

*Mr. Hyde:*
(1) Shortly after he gained control of the Yankees, Steinbrenner showed a definite lack of knowledge of many facets of baseball. In spring training in Florida, for example, he ordered one of his players to wear his cap properly. The player did have his cap on backwards, but he was a catcher!

(2) Shows an extreme lack of tolerance for a player making an error. Once when Bobby Murcer muffed an outfield ground ball in a spring exhibition game, Steinbrenner blurted: "I'm paying him more than $100,000 a year and he can't catch the ball."

(3) Seems to take sadistic pleasure in squashing little people. Once he had the switchboard operator in a Boston hotel fired because she wouldn't allow him to place a long distance call from the telephone in a bar, as per regulations.

(4) Constantly ridicules his top players in public. He has, for example, called Dave Winfield "Mr. May" for ostensibly not performing well in late season stretch drives—and even criticized Don Mattingly for being "selfish" after he hit a record-tying eight homers in eight straight games in 1987. Mattingly injured his wrist shortly after this record string, and Steinbrenner blamed it on Mattingly's "exaggerated home run swing."

(5) Whenever the Yankees begin playing badly, Steinbrenner pushes the panic button and starts firing, or threatening to fire, his managers and pitching coaches. Steinbrenner changed managers at least 14 times since 1973, and has had an uncounted number of pitching coaches. In 1982, when the Yankees finished a dismal fifth in the Eastern Division, Steinbrenner employed three different managers during the season: Bob Lemon, Gene Michael and Clyde King. Before Steinbrenner fires a manager, he usually embarrasses him no end in the public press.


*Dr. Jekyll:*

(1) Steinbrenner may fire his managers as often as some people change their socks, but he ordinarily doesn't kick them out of the Yankees organization. They remain on the payroll either as general manager, super-scout, special assistant, or coach, if they so desire—and at handsome salaries. Ex-Yankee managers who've stayed on with the organization in one capacity or another include: Lou Piniella, Bob Lemon, Gene Michael, Clyde King, and of course, Billy Martin.

(2) In 1979, Steinbrenner led a delegation down to Curacao in the Caribbean in order to assist the Curacao

58

Baseball Federation, both with special instruction and a generous donation of baseball equipment. Yogi Berra and Billy Martin, among others, accompanied Steinbrenner on this little publicized goodwill tour.

(3) Reggie Jackson helped Steinbrenner achieve some of his greatest successes during Reggie's five years with the Yankees (1977–81)—three pennants and two World Series victories—but was let go after 1981 because he was thought to be "over-the-hill." However, after Jackson hit his 500th major league homer with the California Angels in 1984, Steinbrenner presented him with a very expensive sterling silver platter commemorating the event.

(4) Steinbrenner made it a point to make a special trip to Cooperstown in July 1987 to witness Jim "Catfish" Hunter's induction into baseball's Hall of Fame. Steinbrenner signed Hunter as his first major free agent in 1975, and Catfish responded by playing a major role in helping the Yankees capture three American League pennants. No one appreciates true achievement more than George.

(5) George M. Steinbrenner appreciates true achievement in any field. For example, he long admired the work of George E. Seedhouse, Supervisor of Community Centers and Playgrounds in Cleveland, Ohio, during the 1950s and 1960s. And in recognition of that work he named one of his American Shipbuilding Co. iron ore carriers (a 13,000-ton vessel) *George E. Seedhouse.*

# BILL VEECK: BASEBALL'S SHOWMAN EXTRAORDINAIRE

When Bill Veeck (as in "wreck") bought the Cleveland Indians in 1946, he took over a moribund baseball franchise that hadn't fielded a pennant winner since 1920. With an incredible flair for showmanship, he succeeded in boosting the season's attendance to over 1,050,000, shattering all previous Indians' records, though the team never managed to climb out of sixth place that year.

Veeck believed that when fans came to the ball park they

A jubilant Bill Veeck (center) had reason to celebrate in 1948
after his Indians, led by player-manager Lou Boudreau
(right), had trounced the Boston Braves in the World Series.
At left is coach Bill McKechnie. (Photo—Sporting News)

should be entertained *totally*. For starters, he hired several
jazz combos to wander through the stands and perform at
the end of each half-inning.

Next he hired former minor league pitcher Max Patkin,
a contortionist, to coach occasional innings at third base.
One of the strangest-looking characters ever to wear a
baseball uniform, Patkin made it difficult for opposing
pitchers to concentrate on the game as they couldn't help
watching Max twist himself in and out of pretzel shapes
along the coaching lines. Coaches rarely receive applause
of any kind, but the fans howled with glee at the sight
of "Coach" Patkin, and sometimes gave him standing ova-
tions for his outlandish performances.

At about the time Patkin became an Indian, Veeck signed
up 33-year-old minor league infielder and stuntman Jackie
Price as a player-coach. Price pulled off feats never seen

before on a ball field. Among other things, he could throw two or three balls simultaneously and make them all curve, he could catch balls dropped from blimps high in the air, and even play an occasional game of shortstop for Cleveland.

One of Jackie's most memorable stunts was to suspend himself upside down from a 12-foot-high horizontal bar, grab a bat and have balls pitched to him which he hit distances of 150 feet and more. Fans jammed their way into the park to watch Patkin and Price go through their extraordinary acts.

Bill Veeck had operated the Milwaukee Brewers of the American Association with great success in the early 1940s and in recognition of his achievements he was named in 1942 by *The Sporting News* as Minor League Executive of the Year. He was only 28 then. Shortly after his Milwaukee Brewers' exploits, Veeck entered the U.S. Marine Corps, was shipped off to the South Pacific, and while stationed at Bougainville during the height of World War II, sustained a severe injury to his right leg as the result of an artillery training exercise. Unfortunately, the leg never healed properly, but during that hectic summer of '46 Veeck hobbled around through the grandstands daily, talking to the fans and getting their views as to how the Indians could be improved. Numerous times after an arduous day promoting the team, Veeck would writhe in pain at night as his leg flared up.

Infection set in and on November 1, 1946, the leg was amputated nine inches below the knee. Shortly after the operation, Veeck, still under the influence of anesthesia and quite woozy, grabbed the telephone and called Franklin Lewis, sports editor of the *Cleveland Press*, to see how the Indians came out in the major league draft. Baseball was always on his mind.

Veeck was fitted with an artificial leg, but the pain did not disappear, and there were other operations until finally in 1961 he had to have amputation above the knee. During all those years he never permitted physical pain to dim his enthusiasm for baseball. On frequent occasions he removed the artificial leg and amused friends by using it as an ashtray.

"Wild Bill," as he was called by the local writers, used

every sort of promotion imaginable. One night, for example, he would give the ladies orchids specially flown in from Hawaii, and on another night he would have former Olympic track champion Jesse Owens dress up in an Indians uniform and run a foot race against one of his players. Owens, then well into his thirties, generally won.

Unpredictable "Wild Bill" suddenly sold the team (at an enormous profit) and took a year's sabbatical from baseball before he bought the St. Louis Browns in 1951. Veeck used more promotional gimmicks to draw fans into Sportsman's Park to watch his inept Browns in action: He gave away a 200-pound block of ice one night, and another time live lobsters, and in desperation he sent a midget up to the plate to pinch-hit. (See page 16.)

Bill surfaced again when he bought the Chicago White Sox at the end of 1958. He reached his peak as a master showman when he introduced the exploding scoreboard at Chicago's Comiskey Park. Every time a White Sox player hit a homer the scoreboard would erupt into a crescendo of sound and shoot off a fireworks rocket display. Other major league owners were shocked and called it an "outrage," but the fans loved it. Eventually other teams in both leagues installed their own exploding scoreboards.

Veeck was forced to sell the Sox after the 1961 season because of a severe illness. He re-emerged as a big league owner for the fourth and last time in 1975, when he headed a group that again bought the financially ailing White Sox. Next, "Wild Bill" had his team wear short pants during the hot days of summer in 1976. One sportswriter fumed, "The White Sox look like an amateur softball team." However, Veeck at no time allowed his critics to hamper his highly individualistic style of running baseball teams. He spent some of his last years rooting in the bleachers, sitting bare-chested and chatting with the other fans.

Bill Veeck has not yet been named to baseball's Hall of Fame. However, no one during the past half-century has made a greater impact on the baseball scene.

# GAME BORES MANAGER—
# LEAVES BENCH FOR HOT DOG

When Luke Appling was managing the Kansas City Athletics on an interim basis late in the 1967 season, he became so bored with the game that he went up behind the grandstand and ordered a hot dog and beer from a refreshment stand. He didn't come back down into the dugout until he had finished his repast. Result: Appling, an easy-going Southerner, was not invited to manage the Athletics for the 1968 season.

Appling, the Hall of Fame shortstop, who played 20 years for the Chicago White Sox (1930–50), remained in various coaching capacities, however, after his Kansas City experience. He made baseball headlines in 1985 when at the age of 78 he slammed a home run into the leftfield stands at Washington, D.C.'s Robert F. Kennedy Stadium during an Old-Timers' Game.

In 1987, Appling was still listed as batting coach for the Atlanta Braves.

Ted Turner
on Stunt Day.

## TURNER MANAGES HIS
## BRAVES FOR ONE DAY

There had been eccentric team owners before, but when
the flamboyant advertising billboard and television tycoon,
Robert Edward "Ted" Turner III, bought the Atlanta Braves
in 1975, little did the world of baseball realize how strange
the diamond game could become with a completely
uninhibited owner running a major league franchise.

Turner was at his outrageous best during a special "Field
Day" staged at Atlanta Stadium shortly after he took charge
of the Braves when he got down on his hands and knees
and pushed a baseball with his nose from third base to
home plate.

Also in his earlier days as team owner he was often the
star attraction at home games where his rooting from his

private box became so boisterous that fans often paid their way into the park just to see Turner in action. In typical Turner fashion he would settle into his seat, doff his jacket, stuff a plug of chewing tobacco into his face, and bellow "Awwriiight!" every time one of his players batted in a run or made an outstanding play in the field. Or after a foul ball sailed into the seats his celebrated frugal streak became activated as he sighed, "There goes four dollars," and, after three more fouls followed, he groaned "*Sixteen* dollars!"

"Baseballs are expensive"
—Ted Turner

Once his Braves became so deeply mired in the second division that Turner threatened to call up his entire Savannah farm team to replace all his Atlanta regulars.

Early in the 1977 season, Atlanta under manager Dave Bristol began floundering badly and on May 10 the situation reached a climax when the Braves lost their 16th straight game. Turner could stand it no longer, so he ordered Bristol to go off on a 10-day "scouting trip" and appointed himself manager. On May 11 tempestuous Ted donned a uniform, ensconced himself in the dugout between two of his most trusted coaches (Eddie Haas and Vic Correll), and formally took over the reins as Braves pilot.

His players cringed at the sight of Turner in uniform because they knew his knowledge of the game's techniques was severely limited. For example, in his first days as owner, as his deputies explained the rudiments of baseball to him, Turner blurted, "What the hell is a bunt?" Despite the cringing and grumbling of his players, Turner called the shots for the entire game—with the assistance of his coaches—but he could do no better than Bristol as the Braves proceeded to lose their 17th straight game (to Pittsburgh) 2-1.

Most of the nation's baseball fans laughed at this moment of comic relief and Turner felt himself ready to manage for a while longer. However, National League President Charles S. Feeney was not amused and advised Turner that he was in violation of Major League Rule 20 which states in part: "No manager or player on a club shall directly or indirectly own stock or have any financial interest in the club by which he is employed except under an agreement approved by the commissioner . . ."

Commissioner Bowie Kuhn refused to give such approval and Ted Turner's managerial career ended after a single game in the dugout.

In that 1977 season Atlanta finished dead last in the National League's West Division with a dismal 61-101 record, but Ted Turner is still officially listed in all the standard baseball record books as being manager for a day with an 0-1 record.

# WALT ALSTON GOES DOWN SWINGING IN HIS ONLY AT-BAT IN MAJORS

Walter "Smokey" Alston, who managed the Brooklyn-Los Angeles Dodgers for 23 years (1954–76), winning 2,040 regular season games, came to bat only one solitary time as a big leaguer. Called up from Huntington, West Virginia of the Middle Atlantic League by the St. Louis Cardinals for the proverbial "cup-of-coffee" in September, 1936, he got into a game against the Chicago Cubs when regular first baseman Johnny Mize was ejected in the eighth inning for arguing with the umpire.

Alston, a powerful righthanded slugger who had belted 35 homers for Huntington, faced the Cubs star righthander, Lon Warneke, took three hard swings and struck out. We must hasten to add, however, that Alston's middle strike was a vicious foul liner down the leftfield line. In the field in the ninth, Alston cleanly handled one chance, but booted a grounder, and wound up with a lifetime fielding average in the majors of .500.

Alston continued playing in the minors through the mid-1940s, but Branch Rickey, wise old general manager of the Brooklyn Dodgers, recognized his potential as a manager early on and assigned him to pilot various Dodger farm clubs, including Nashua, St. Paul and Montreal.

Finally, in 1954, Alston was called up to the major leagues for the second time, but this time as a manager he stuck. In 1955, he led the Dodgers to their only World Championship in Brooklyn and to a pennant in 1956 before the team moved to the West Coast. In Los Angeles his clubs captured world titles in 1959, 1963 and 1965 and pennants in 1966 and 1974.

In 1983, Walter Alston became the tenth manager to gain election to baseball's Hall of Fame at Cooperstown.

# FROM BOSWELL TO
# BASEBALL: THE CASE
# OF PRESIDENT GIAMATTI

A. Bartlett Giamatti, former president of Yale University and president of the National League since January 1, 1987, has brought a touch of class to baseball—he is the first authentic academician to hold a high administrative post in baseball's hierarchy.

Born in Boston on April 4, 1938, Giamatti developed a passion for baseball as a youngster and dreamed of some day becoming a member of the Boston Red Sox. Above all, he wanted to emulate his favorite Bosox player, Bobby Doerr.

His true talent, however, lay in the groves of academe, and in 1960 he graduated with a B.A. *magna cum laude* from Yale University. He continued on at Yale's Graduate School, winning his Ph.D. in comparative literature in 1964, after submitting a doctoral dissertation entitled *The Earthly Paradise in the Renaissance Epic*. Along the way Giamatti also studied under Yale's Professor F. A. Pottle, the renowned authority on the work of James Boswell, the biographer of lexicographer Samuel Johnson.

Giamatti taught at Princeton for a year and then returned to Yale in 1965 as an assistant professor of English and Comparative Literature. Giamatti almost immediately became a shining star on the Yale faculty and published a number of scholarly books, including: *Plays of Double Senses: Spenser's Faerie Queene* (1975), *The University and the Public Interest* (1981) and *Exile and Change in Renaissance Literature* (1984).

In 1978, at the age of 40, he was chosen as president of Yale University, becoming one of the youngest major university chief executives in the United States. Giamatti, however, was still a Boston Red Sox fan at heart and remarked just before his formal inauguration, "I'd much rather be President of the *American* League."

During his days as Yale prexy, Giamatti was often seen walking along the campus wearing rumpled slacks, a sports jacket and a Boston Red Sox cap to go along with a beard labelled by *Newsweek* as "slightly satanic."

After little more than eight years at Yale's helm, Giamatti resigned his high academic post upon being elected president of the National League. Though he would have preferred the A.L., Giamatti reasoned: "Baseball beckoned, and a major league is a major league."

A league president is faced with myriad administrative tasks, many of them very difficult, and in this connection we interviewed Giamatti just prior to the July 14 major league All-Star game played at Oakland's Alameda County Coliseum. In commenting about his N.L. duties in general, Giamatti said:

"Determining legalities and illegalities in player contracts can be an extremely complex task. I can recall Yale professors translating cuneiform writing on Babylonian clay tablets in the Sterling Library dating back 4,000 years. I won't say that multi-page player contracts are as difficult to comprehend as cuneiform, but some come awfully close. I've also spent a lot of time reviewing the ins and outs of the balk rule. People keep asking me why National League umpires are calling so many balks this year, and in response I just tell them that the pitchers are committing more balks. Period."

At an All-Star game press conference at Oakland, Giamatti exhibited his sharp wit when a California sportswriter asked him: "Because there are so many home runs being hit in 1987, do you think the baseballs have been juiced up?"

"The baseballs are not juiced up any more than I am," retorted Giamatti. He went on to say:

"Naturally, I'm concerned with the baseball quality question because I've got my signature on every ball used in the National League."

In a study conducted by both major leagues, it was determined that the baseballs used in 1987 were no livelier than those put into play in previous years.

# 4. TOUGH PITCHERS

## NOLAN RYAN: KING OF ZING

Nolan Ryan in 1987, at the age of 40 and in his 20th year in the major leagues, enjoyed one of his finest seasons on the mound despite the fact that he went 8-16 for the Houston Astros. Regardless of that losing record, the righthanded fireballer led the National League in strikeouts with 270 and in ERA with a very low 2.76. Since Ryan pitched only 212 innings, he averaged more than 11 strikeouts per game.

Up to this point, any pitcher who has led the National League in both strikeouts and ERA has taken the Cy Young award. Ryan didn't win the 1987 Cy Young award because of the 8-16 posting, but many baseball observers strongly felt he should have received it despite the .333 won-lost percentage. In those 16 losses, the weak-hitting Astros scored exactly 12 runs while Ryan was on the mound. Nolan should have "sued" his teammates for nonsupport.

Though Nolan Ryan has reached an age when most other pitchers survive by resorting to knuckleballs, spitballs, sandpaper or prayer, he seems to have lost little or nothing on his fastball as he consistently throws in the high 90s. He remains the king of zing. His *changeup,* according to Los Angeles Dodgers speed-gun operator Mike Brito, clocks in at 87 or 88 m.p.h., a bit faster than Fernando Valenzuela's fastball.

"No one throws as fast as Ryan," said Dodgers infielder Phil Garner. "Dwight Gooden of the Mets throws the ball real good, but it doesn't explode on you like Nolan's. His looks like it picks up speed as it comes to the plate."

Ryan's 4,547 lifetime strikeouts through 1987 are far and away a major league record and he looks forward to pitching at least several more years in the majors—and run his K total up to 5,000, an astounding number.

"Certainly 1987 was an unusual year for me since I won only 8 games despite all those strikeouts and a low ERA, but there are some things in baseball you just can't explain," Ryan told reporters at season's end.

This writer interviewed Nolan Ryan in March, 1985, in Florida before a spring training game and asked: "How is it that you've been able to maintain your great speed in your late thirties while most power pitchers lose their velocity fairly early in their careers?"

Ryan answered without batting an eye: "I guess it must be because I'm from Texas." Ryan, a native of Refugio, Texas, makes his home in Alvin, a few miles south of Houston, where he engages in cattle breeding and in banking.

# FASTEST PITCHER?
# RYAN 100.9 MPH,
# DALKOWSKI 108

According to the "Guinness Book of World Records," the fastest recorded *major league pitcher* is Nolan Ryan, who, on August 20, 1974, while with the California Angels, threw a pitch at Anaheim Stadium, California, measured at 100.9 miles per hour.

Steve Dalkowski, little-known lefthander (b. June 3, 1939), though not generally regarded as the fastest pitcher in baseball history, threw a pitch measured at 108 miles per hour while with Elmira in the Class A Eastern League in 1962.

Dalkowski spent nine years in the minor leagues (1957–65), mostly as a Baltimore Orioles farmhand, reaching as high as Rochester and Columbus of the International League, but his wildness prevented his promotion to the majors. He was invited to spring training several times by the Orioles, but never reached his true potential though he possessed an enormous amount of raw talent.

In those nine years in the minors, Dalkowski put together one of the strangest pitching records in professional baseball history. Over the course of 236 games, he posted a 46-80 won-lost record (.366 percentage) and pitched 995 innings, allowing only 682 base hits. He walked the Gargantuan total of 1,354 batters and struck out an equally Gargantuan 1,396. His ERA was a rather bloated 5.59.

Thus, in a typical game Dalkowski gave up 6 hits, walked 12 and struck out 12 to 13. If he went the distance, his game almost always took more than three hours to complete, and no one who ever paid his way into a game pitched by Steve Dalkowski ever complained about not getting his money's worth. Every game he pitched was a dramatic event.

While with Stockton of the Class A California League in 1960, he pitched 170 innings in 32 games, won 7 games, lost 15, allowed only 105 hits, walked 262 and struck out 262! Obviously he was very hard to hit.

Dalkowski's great left arm began giving out before he was 27, and from that point on, his journey through life was not altogether happy. He worked for a time as a migratory laborer in California's vineyards and had long bouts with John Barleycorn.

In 1978, the Society for American Baseball Research (then based in Cooperstown, New York) honored Dalkowski by including him in a newly published biographical and statistical volume entitled *All-Time Minor League Baseball Stars*.

# SPITBALL PITCHER SPAT IN UMPIRE'S FACE!

After Burleigh Grimes ended his active career in the majors, he became player-manager for Bloomington in the Three-I League in 1935. Burleigh was barely at the midpoint of his professional baseball career at this juncture. He managed Louisville in the American Association in 1936 and then he led the Brooklyn Dodgers in 1937–38. Grimes held the reins at Brooklyn between the managerial tenures of Casey Stengel and Leo Durocher.

After directing Montreal in the International League in 1939, Grimes somehow went down a couple of steps on the managerial ladder in 1940 when he was named pilot of Grand Rapids in the Class C Michigan State League. And it was in his Grand Rapids tenure that he endured the worst experience in his professional baseball career spanning nearly three-score years.

In early July, Grimes took his Grand Rapids Colts down to Flint for a crucial game in the Michigan State League pennant race, but from the very start Burleigh became dissatisfied with the calls of home plate umpire Bob Williams. Toward the late innings, Grimes could take it no more and embroiled himself in a violent argument with Williams. In fact, the old spitballer became so exasperated that he ran out of words and vented his anger and spat out his entire chaw of tobacco smack into Williams' face.

Williams, naturally enough, promptly ejected Grimes from the game, and a few days later, on July 7th, Judge William G. Bramham, president of the National Association of Professional Baseball Leagues (the governing body of minor league baseball) did Williams one better by suspending Grimes for an entire year.

The suspension took effect from the date of the offense and thus any plans Grimes had for managing in 1941 had to be scrapped. In being banished from organized baseball for a full year, Grimes took the stiffest punishment a manager had ever received up to that point. (In September, 1942, Judge Bramham suspended manager Ben Chapman of Richmond in the Piedmont League for a full year for slugging an umpire.)

Grimes, who fought the suspension, had plenty of support from his many friends in baseball, and during the lengthy hearings on the case, umpire Bob Williams was suspended for "inefficiency" and "for the good of the league," but he was later reinstated in good standing.

In recalling the incident more than 40 years later, Grimes, as he sat in a comfortable easy chair in the Otesaga lobby, said softly: "It was a hot day, the game was going badly, the umpire, in my estimation, was making a lot of bad calls, and I just lost my head momentarily. I shouldn't have done it . . . and it really cost me."

Grimes, professional all the way, got back into the game in 1942 as manager of Toronto in the International League for the first of his three tours of duty there: 1942-44, 1947 and 1952-53. He managed Rochester, also in the I.L., in

1945–46, with his final assignment in uniform coming in 1955 when he coached the Kansas City Athletics.

Then he served several long stints as a scout for a number of teams, including the New York Yankees, Kansas City A's and the Baltimore Orioles. The latter assignment stretched from 1960 to 1971, Burleigh's last full-time job in baseball. He had made the rounds.

During the last dozen or so years of his long life, Burleigh Grimes worked actively on the Hall of Fame's Committee on Baseball Veterans, and enjoyed some of his best days holding court at the Otesaga lobby during Hall of Fame Induction Ceremony time. Reporters came flocking to him with pads, pencils and tape recorders to seek his views on everything from the art of throwing the spitball to historic games he was involved in generations ago.

Hall of Famer Burleigh Grimes, ordinarily a good-hitting pitcher, once made 8 outs in a single game on only 4 at-bats—he hit into a triple play, two double plays and struck out!

# GEORGE BLAEHOLDER, FATHER OF THE SLIDER

George Blaeholder ran up a mediocre 104-125 record as a righthanded pitcher in the American League from 1925 to 1936, but he is credited with having been the first pitcher to throw the slider, one of the most difficult of all pitches to hit. He threw his first slider with the St. Louis Browns in 1928, and generously passed on his technique to other pitchers.

The slider takes off like a fastball, but then curves sharply just before it reaches the batter. Batters have scornfully referred to the slider as a "nickel curve." The pitch really didn't have a major impact upon baseball until the 1950s and 1960s.

Stan Musial, one of the greatest batters of all time (he banged out 3,630 base hits and averaged .331 in a 23-year career, 1941–63), once said: "I could have hit better in the latter years of my career and stayed around a while longer if it hadn't been for the slider."

# PITCHES FOR 23 TEAMS
# IN 13 LEAGUES DURING
# A 27-YEAR CAREER

In an active baseball career that spanned 27 years (1924–50), Walter "Boom-Boom" Beck, a native of Decatur, Illinois, spent a good deal of his time traveling as he pitched for a total of 23 teams in 13 different leagues, including both major leagues. In addition to his American and National League experience, Beck toiled in the following circuits that are obscure to many fans: Three-I League, Texas Association, Western League, American Association, International League, Southern Association, Pacific Coast League, Inter-State League, Southeast League, Central League and Middle Atlantic League. In the latter three leagues he was a player-manager.

As a major leaguer the righthanded-throwing Beck saw action with the St. Louis Browns, Brooklyn Dodgers, Philadelphia Phillies, Detroit Tigers, Cincinnati Reds and Pittsburgh Pirates, and posted a 38-69 record in 265 games. In the minors, he went 199-167, making his total pro regular season record come to just one victory over .500, or 237-236.

Beck enjoyed his finest season in the minors with the Memphis Chicks in 1932 when he rolled up an impressive 27-6 mark to rank as the leading pitcher in the Southern Association. This earned him a return trip to the big leagues in 1933, this time with Brooklyn, and it was in Flatbush that Beck earned his unusual nickname.

While pitching against the Phillies on a sweltering 1934 afternoon in Philadelphia's Baker Bowl, Beck was removed from the game by manager Casey Stengel while still holding a slim lead. Losing his cool, Beck wound up and threw the ball with all his strength toward rightfield where it made a resounding "boom" as it struck the tin fence. Outfielder Hack Wilson, who had not been paying attention during the pitching change, heard the "boom" and, thinking the ball was in play, fielded it and made a perfect line throw to second base. This unusual episode caused all the fans and players, except for Beck, to laugh heartily. From that time on Walter Beck was known as "Boom-Boom." Hack Wilson, a Hall of Famer, who had his best season in the majors with the Chicago Cubs when he hit 56 homers and knocked in 190 runs (the all-time major league record) was then in the twilight of his career and found himself released by the Dodgers to the Phillies later in the 1934 season.

After his playing days were over, "Boom-Boom" Beck remained in baseball for another two decades as a coach and scout at both the major and minor league levels. He died at Champaign, Illinois, on May 7, 1987, at the age of 82.

# IT DIDN'T PAY TO MESS WITH BURLY EARLY WYNN

Early Wynn, the Hall of Fame righthander who piled up a 300-244 won-lost record over 23 big league seasons (1939–63, with time out for World War II service), looked as mean as a junkyard dog when he took the mound. He had his own special way of intimidating hitters. Most batters were afraid to dig in on "Burly Early" because they never knew when his brush-back pitch was coming.

One reporter commented that Early would knock down his own grandmother if she ever crowded the plate—fortunately, she never had the opportunity of batting against her grandson. However, when Early was nearing the end of the trail with the Chicago White Sox in the early 1960s, he pitched against his 17-year-old son Early, Jr., in batting practice. Well, Early, Jr., socked one of his dad's best pitches up against the bleacher wall. What do you suppose happened when the boy dug in for his father's next delivery? He was sent flying on his derrière, of course, in order to avoid the high hard one.

One time Early was asked to name the toughest batter he ever faced. Wynn replied without a moment's hesitation, "There were two guys . . . one was named Hillerich and the other was Bradsby."

That meant Early's enemy was anyone with a bat in his hands.

# 5. TOUGH BATTERS

## TY COBB:
## LONG BALL HITTER AND
## TIGER ON THE BASE PATHS

"Ty Cobb is absolutely the greatest ballplayer I've ever seen on the diamond, and that includes everyone I've either played with or against," declared Joe Sewell, Hall of Fame infielder, in an interview conducted in the summer of 1987 at Cooperstown's Hotel Otesaga.

Sewell went on to say:

"When not in uniform, Ty Cobb personified the true Southern gentleman, but once he put on the Detroit flannels, he seemed to change character, almost like a Jekyll and Hyde. He played every inning of every game as if it were the critical point of a World Series . . . . Even when he took his position in the outfield, he appeared like a tiger ready to spring.

"When he came roaring into second base on a close play, or to break up a double play, he reminded me of a runaway locomotive. He loudly proclaimed that the base line belonged to him and felt justified in running over any infielder who got in his way. But anyone who saw me play knows I didn't bail out when Cobb barreled into second base. I gave him as much as he gave me."

No question about that because Sewell, who stood only 5 feet 7 inches and weighed 160 pounds, had the reputation of being a very scrappy and aggressive shortstop (later in his career he switched over to third base). He made up for his lack of size with his own special brand of ferocity.

In continuing to recall Ty Cobb's exploits on the baseball diamond, Sewell said:

"When I played against Cobb in the 1920s, he was getting well on into his thirties, but age didn't stop him a bit from being a demon on the base paths. Remember that

Cobb was never the fastest runner in baseball, not even when he came up to the Tigers as a kid in 1905. But he knew *how* to run because he studied how to stride properly . . . he learned to cut yards off the distance between bases by knowing how to make sharp turns and how to tag the bag on the inside. He ran in straight lines. How many times do you see players today making wide turns and running any number of unnecessary yards in circling the bases?

"Sure, I pick Ty Cobb as the greatest ballplayer of all time, even ahead of Babe Ruth," Joe Sewell pontificated without a noticeable trace of doubt in his voice. "Remember that I played against Ruth during his peak years . . . and I was his teammate on the Yankees in the early 1930s when he was still going good. Ruth hit all those home runs, but Cobb could whack the ball as hard as anyone. I know firsthand because I caught lots of his drives that nearly broke my hand.

"The sportswriters began getting on Cobb in the mid-1920s because he was still content to hit singles and doubles when the home run was just coming into vogue. So he decided to show everyone he could match Ruth or anyone else for power. If I remember correctly, it was at St. Louis' Sportsman's Park in early May 1925 that Cobb decided to take a full swing and put on a real power exhibition. In the first game of the series, he went six for six and clubbed three homers, and on the next he hammered two more homers—that was five in two days and enough to tie the major league record. As I recall he got two doubles in those two games that nearly cleared the wall. He just missed *seven* homers in two days.

"Then Cobb went back to his natural snap swing batting style, but he proved his point that hitting home runs was no great trick."

# JOE SEWELL: "IRON MAN," A TOUGH BATTER TO STRIKE OUT

Joe Sewell broke into the big leagues under both tragic and dramatic circumstances. He was called up by the Cleveland Indians from the New Orleans Pelicans of the Southern Association on August 18, 1920, the day after their regular shortstop, Ray Chapman, was killed by a pitch thrown by the New York Yankees submarine artist Carl Mays at the Polo Grounds, New York. Chapman is the only player in major league history to have been killed during the course of a game.

Sewell stepped right into the shortstop slot and, with his timely hitting and good fielding, helped the Indians capture both the American League pennant and a World Series victory over the Brooklyn Dodgers.

Sewell remained with the Indians through 1930, playing mostly at shortstop, and then spent the final three years of his career with the New York Yankees as a third baseman. In 14 years of big league action, Sewell, a left-handed hitter, banged out 2,226 base hits in 1,903 games and had a batting average of .312, a sound enough record to earn him Hall of Fame election in 1977.

Amazingly enough, Sewell struck out only 114 times in those 14 years, in over 8,000 total plate appearances (including walks, sacrifices, etc.). He whiffed but three times in both 1930 and 1932, and he struck out only four times in three other seasons—and all these were when he was a regular playing in well over 100 games per year.

Joe Sewell is the all-time big league champion in being the toughest man to strike out.

When we spoke with Sewell in July 1987 in Cooperstown, we asked him why so many of today's hitters are fanning so frequently, pointing out that some of them roll up 114 strikeouts even before the season winds into August.

"Because they don't keep their eye on the ball!" snapped the 89-year-old Sewell, who is still very much alert, sharp-tongued and sharp-minded. "Too many batters today swing wildly trying for the home run instead of just going with the pitch and meeting the ball. If you're talking about *strange baseball*, it's strange to me why so many contemporary players lack discipline and refuse to control their swings the way they should."

Sewell added:

"Don't forget that the pitchers I faced in the 1920s and 1930s were just as fast as the ones throwing today. I faced flame throwers like Walter Johnson and Lefty Grove and they had a hard time striking me out because I had a compact swing and watched the ball the whole way. It's hard for me to imagine that legions of batters in the 1980s are striking out 125 to 150 times and more per season and not getting farmed out."

That may be because they have million-dollar contracts.

Joe Sewell was an authentic "Iron Man" of his day, playing in 1,103 consecutive games from 1922 to 1928. At that time Sewell's Iron Man performance ranked second only to that of Everett Scott, American League infielder who played in 1,307 games in a row from 1916 to 1925. Even now Sewell's streak ranks as No. 5 on the all-time list. Lou Gehrig stands No. 1, of course, with his staggering total of 2,130 straight games.

When asked why his streak came to a halt at 1,103, Sewell replied: "One morning I got up and found out I had the flu real bad and so I had to crawl right back into bed. Still, no one made a big fuss about playing streaks 50-60 years ago. At that time my 1,103 straight games plus a dime would be good for a cup of coffee."

(Cal Ripken, Jr., Baltimore Orioles shortstop, established a big league record by playing 8,243 consecutive *innings* over the course of 908 games, but was pulled out in the eighth inning on a September 14, 1987 game by his father, manager Cal Ripken, Sr., who said: "I wanted to get everybody to stop writing about the consecutive inning streak. The media pressure on us was getting intense, and so we just had to put an end to the streak.")

Sewell also recalled: "Lifetime records didn't attract all that much attention in the old days. I remember when Tris Speaker, our manager and centerfielder at Cleveland, got base hit Number 3,000 in 1925 . . . there was hardly a ripple about it. The newspapers made passing mention of this milestone, but 'Spoke' received nothing in the way of special tributes."

Clifford Kachline, former Hall of Fame Historian and longtime baseball writer, commented that Ty Cobb received relatively little publicity when he lined out base hit No. 4,000 while playing for the Philadelphia A's in 1927.

"Just check Cobb's file in the Hall of Fame Library and you won't see any banner headlines about that milestone," Kachline said.

Also there's no record of the President in 1927 calling from the Oval Office in the White House to congratulate Cobb. When Pete Rose broke Stan Musial's National League base hit record of 3,630, Ronald Reagan got right on the White House phone to call Rose before Pete had a chance to take his post-game shower. And when Rose got hit Number 4,192 in 1985 to pass Ty Cobb on the all-time list, Mr. Reagan got on the White House phone again to congratulate Pete.

"Everybody is statistics-happy today, even the President of the United States," muttered Joe Sewell.

# PETE ROSE:
# SLUGGER BEGAN AT AGE 3, WASTED VALUABLE YEARS IN HIGH SCHOOL

Pete Rose's father Harry was anxious to get his first-born son started in baseball at the earliest possible age, so little Pete began at just 2 years to catch thrown balls. When Pete was 3 he started out as a slugger. The first time he remembers slugging he connected solidly with a pitch served up by his dad, and drove a hard rubber-coated ball to right centerfield, over and out of the backyard ball field and against a glass windowpane that promptly cracked in the kitchen of the Rose home on Braddock Avenue in Cincinnati.

That long drive by the Cincinnati Red, who holds

"What a boy, what a batter, that Pete."

baseball's all-time career record of 4,256 hits, was swatted on a summer Saturday in 1944. The crack is still in the window. According to a July 7, 1987, *New York Times* report, LaVerne Noeth, Pete's mother, was standing in the kitchen that day more than four decades ago when she heard the glass crack.

"My husband said, 'Hon, come here, look where Pete hit the ball,'" Mrs. Noeth recalled recently. "He said, 'I don't want it fixed. I'm going to show people where he hit that ball.' Pete was so small then, he was always small."

Little has changed in the neighborhood. Braddock Avenue is still a clump of homes on a hill above the Ohio River, five miles west of downtown, and boys still play ball there. At the old Rose household, members of Pete's family have no trouble finding first base in the backyard although the ball field is now covered with honeysuckle shrubs and black locust trees.

But the cracked window may soon disappear: the house is for sale. If anyone repairs that window, a slice of Americana will be lost.

After he hit that storied backyard liner at the age of 3, Pete Rose continued playing ball at a furious pace, and he became so involved in various sandlot leagues that it took him five years to get through high school in Cincinnati. By having to spend that extra year, Pete didn't start his pro career with Geneva, N.Y. of the New York-Penn League until he was 19 in 1960, when others began at 18.

If he had started in the minors a year earlier, he might have had an additional season in the big leagues and broken even more records. Pete didn't fail in high school because he was a bad student, mind you. His I.Q. had been measured as high as 150.

# BABE RUTH: BEATS WHOLE AMERICAN LEAGUE IN HOME RUN PRODUCTION

Home run hitting clearly reached its peak in the major leagues in 1987 as a record number of players (27) hit for the circuit 30 or more times. Although there are so many sluggers going for homers, still there is no single slugger who dominates the long ball game as Babe Ruth did during the 1920s.

Ruth, in fact, on two separate occasions, in 1920 and 1927, personally hit more homers than each of the seven other *teams* in the American League. In 1920, the "Sultan of Swat" smacked out a record 54 homers and no *team* in the league matched that total. St. Louis came the closest with 50, followed by Philadelphia with 44; Chicago, 37; Washington, 36; Cleveland, 35; Detroit, 30; and Boston, 22.

In 1927, the Bambino reached the peak of his long ball power as he whacked a record 60 homers, and that year no single A.L. team managed to top that total. Philadelphia "threatened" Ruth with 56 four baggers, followed by St. Louis with 55; Detroit, 51; Chicago, 36; Washington, 29; Boston, 28; and Cleveland, 26.

No other major league player has come close to matching this particular home run achievement of George Herman Ruth.

Most veteran baseball observers believe that no one could hit a baseball harder or farther than Babe Ruth when he was at his peak with the New York Yankees from 1920 to the early 1930s. Ruth's longest homer may well have been a 600-foot shot he belted in a spring exhibition game at Tampa in 1925.

No one ever measured the velocity of his drives, but pitcher Mel Harder who came up with the Cleveland Indians in 1928 recalled the days when the Bambino batted against him at Cleveland's old League Park. This vintage-style ball park (now torn down) had a concrete wall topped by a wire fence running from rightfield to right centerfield. "Ruth's drives often hit that concrete rightfield wall with such tremendous force that the ball would bounce all the way back to second base," Harder said. "Those balls would usually have to be thrown out of the game because they came back a bit flattened and carried a spot of green paint from the wall," he added.

# JIMMIE FOXX AND MICKEY MANTLE: WHO HIT BALL HARDER?

If Jimmie Foxx had stuck more closely to training rules, he could have piled up even more impressive statistics, for through the 1940 season, when he was only 33, he had already smashed out an even 500 homers. From that point on, he was only able to hit 34 more in the big leagues.

Foxx stood an even 6 feet in height, weighed about 210 pounds, and was proportioned like a Charles Atlas with a massive chest and powerful forearms. Called "The Beast" because of his enormous strength (he developed his physique as a Maryland farm boy), he could hit homers righthanded as far as Babe Ruth could hit them lefthanded.

As a member of the Boston Red Sox in 1938, he lined a shot to the deepest corner of the leftfield bleachers at

Cleveland's Municipal Stadium 435 feet away. Lots of hitters can blast baseballs 435 feet, but Foxx's line drive had so much velocity behind it that it broke the back of a wooden seat at that great distance!

On one occasion in batting practice Foxx hit a drive back to the box with such force that the pitcher could not get his glove up in time to shield himself (as Mark Eichhorn was able to do), and suffered a fractured skull. This particular pitcher, a promising youngster, saw his career ended on that fateful day.

Billy Martin once said Mickey Mantle could hit a baseball harder than anyone he ever saw . . . that may be true, but Martin never saw Ruth and Foxx in action. In deference to Mantle, however, his greatest moment of glory in the power department came on May 30, 1955, at Griffith Stadium when he faced Washington's Pedro Ramos.

Mantle, a switch-hitter batting lefthanded, caught hold of one of Ramos' fastballs and propelled an immensely high drive that appeared to have enough power behind it to clear the rightfield roof, a feat that no player had accomplished in the stadium's half-century history. None of the great sluggers of baseball had even come close to powering a fair ball over the giant-sized filigree, the ornamental work hanging from the lip of the stands, which, in both rightfield and leftfield, hooks into fair territory toward the bleachers. Mantle hit the filigree, and as Joe Reichler, Associated Press baseball writer, who witnessed the drive, said: "He came so close to making history that he still made it. The ball struck high on the facade, barely a foot or two below the edge of the roof . . . For years after that spring 1955 game, fans who came to Griffith Stadium lifted their eyes and stared at the spot where the ball hit. Likely many of them remembered the 565-foot homer Mantle hit in Washington two years before. Unobstructed, the drive against Ramos would have traveled even further."

# JOE DIMAGGIO:
# ALWAYS ONE TOUGH HOMBRE
# TO STRIKE OUT

Most baseball experts feel that the greatest single achievement in baseball was Joe DiMaggio's hitting in 56 straight games in 1941. We beg to differ on this point—in our opinion, Joe D's most remarkable accomplishment was striking out only 369 times in his major league career in approximately 8,000 total times at bat (including walks, sac flies, hit by pitcher, etc.).

Amazingly enough, Joltin' Joe hit 361 homers in his 13 years with the New York Yankees (1936–51, with three years out for World War II military service), a figure only 8 fewer than his total strikeouts! In his rookie year, DiMag fanned on 39 occasions, and he never again struck out that many times in a season.

From that point on, DiMaggio enjoyed six seasons in which he had more homers than K's. Here are the fantastic figures, with homers first and strikeouts second: 1937—46, 37; 1938—32, 21; 1939—30, 20; 1940—31, 30; 1941—30, 13; 1946—25, 24; and 1948—39, 30. The "Yankee Clipper" almost made it again in 1950 when he slammed 32 homers against 33 strikeouts.

Even Bob Feller, baseball's unrivaled strikeout king from the mid-1930s through the 1940s, had a tough time fanning DiMaggio. Joe D, who had a career batting average of better than .320 against Feller, told us recently:

"Feller is best known for his great fastball, of course, but he also had a wicked curve which made him extremely effective. At the same time, he was a proud man and never tried too many curves against me . . . He almost always tried to blow the fastball by me—and since I pretty much knew what to expect I never had too much trouble with him."

We should emphasize here that DiMaggio never struck out much against anybody because he had extremely quick reflexes, perfect coordination and keen eyesight.

## What Righthanded Batter Last Hit .380 or Better? Joe D in 1939

When Joe DiMaggio, New York Yankees centerfielder, won the American League batting championship with a .381 average in 1939, he became the last righthanded hitter in the major leagues to hit .380 or better. Joe played in only 120 games in 1939 because he held out for more than a month at the beginning of the season. He finally settled for a contract calling for $30,000, a small fraction of what he could earn if he were playing today. All baseball salary comparisons are strange.

# MIZE AND TED WILLIAMS VERY TOUGH TO STRIKE OUT

Three times in his career Johnny Mize posted records where his homers topped the totals of his whiffs. While with the New York Giants in 1947, the big lefthanded-hitting first baseman bashed a career high 51 homers and fanned only 42 times—and in the following year he hit for the circuit 40 times against only 37 strikeouts.

In 1950, as a member of the New York Yankees, Mize homered 25 times against 24 strikeouts. Overall, in a 15-year big league career (1936–53, with three years out for World War II military service), Mize rang up 359 homers against 524 strikeouts, an excellent ratio.

"I never swung crazy," Mize told us recently. "If the pitch was out of the strike zone, I just didn't go for it . . . I always tried to wait for my pitch," he disclosed.

Ted Williams, who possessed extraordinary vision, and who knew how to control a bat as well as anyone in baseball, had four seasons in which his homers out-numbered his strikeouts. In this listing the homers are given first: 1941—37, 27; 1950—28, 21; 1953—13, 10; and 1958—28, 24. Overall, in a 19-year career (1939-60, with three years out for World War II military service), Williams hit 524 homers as opposed to 709 strikeouts, a superb ratio.

# BILL DICKEY: DIDN'T TAKE MANY THIRD STRIKES EITHER

Bill Dickey, the Hall of Fame New York Yankees catcher, is another throwback to an earlier era when some of the game's top power hitters were hard to fan. Though he didn't hit as many homers as DiMaggio, Mize or Williams, he still managed to have five seasons when his homers exceeded his strikeouts, and once when they were even (1933—14 and 14.)

Those five sterling Dickey seasons are (homers first): 1932—15, 13; 1935—14, 11; 1936—22, 16; 1937—29, 22; and 1938—27, 22. In 17 seasons with the Yankees (1928–46, with two years out for World War II military service), Bill Dickey rapped out 202 homers against only 289 strikeouts.

Said Dickey recently: "In many ways baseball today is strange to me because so many big-leaguers—or supposed big-leaguers—are lunging at the ball in trying to get distance—and they're striking out 3, 4 and even 5 times a game in the process."

# "SHOELESS" JOE JACKSON: MORE TRIPLES THAN STRIKEOUTS

While with the Chicago White Sox in 1920, Joe Jackson accomplished a feat that would be virtually impossible for a modern player to match—he actually had more triples than strikeouts, 20 to 14. While with the Cleveland Indians in 1912, "Shoeless" Joe lined out 26 triples, but we don't know if his three-baggers outnumbered his whiffs because strikeout records were not kept until 1913.

Compared to Joe Jackson, Dale Mitchell, who was active from 1946 to 1956, was a "modern" player in the strict sense. In any event, Mitchell was the last major leaguer, according to our best calculations, to triple more times than strike out in a single season. While with the Cleveland Indians in 1949, Mitchell, lefthanded slap hitter, tripled 23 times against only 11 strikeouts, a better than a 2-1 ratio. Fantastic!

Sam Crawford, the all-time triples leader with 312, had one season we know about where his three-baggers exceeded his strikeouts: 1916—13, 10. ("Wahoo Sam" was with the Detroit Tigers at the time). Crawford may have had other triples-over-whiffs seasons, but Crawford's strikeout totals while he was with Cincinnati and Detroit from 1899 through 1912 were not kept.

Ty Cobb may have had at least one triples-over-whiffs season, but his 1907–1912 strikeout figures also are shrouded in mystery.

# DON MATTINGLY: HITS WITH EXTRA OOMPH, SETS TWO HOMER RECORDS IN 1987

Don Mattingly has been noted primarily for his fielding and his high batting average. He smashes hard' line drives to every part of the field, with home runs merely a secondary affair until 1987. In his first four seasons with the New York Yankees (1983–86) Mattingly, a 5-foot-11-inch 185-pound lefthanded swinger, belted a good, not great, 93 homers, while batting the lofty average of .332.

In 1987, Mattingly continued his usual high batting average and modest home run-hitting pace. But, while hitting 30 homers, Mattingly, extraordinarily enough, was able to both tie and break two all-time major league home run records.

In July, he hit for the circuit in eight consecutive games, tying the major league mark established by Pittsburgh's Dale Long in 1956. Then on September 29 at Yankee Stadium against Boston he whacked his sixth grand slammer of the season, breaking the record of five that had been shared by Ernie Banks of the Chicago Cubs (1955) and Jim Gentile of the Baltimore Orioles (1961). Oddly,

Mattingly had never hit a grand slammer before the 1987 season.

Mattingly's record-breaking sixth grandslammer came in the third inning off Boston lefthander Bruce Hurst. The ball carried 11 rows into the third tier of the rightfield stands and powered the Yankees to a 6-0 victory over the Red Sox.

Mattingly had never hit Hurst well in the past, averaging a mere .217 with no homers.

When questioned by reporters after the game about his grand slam homer splurge, Mattingly modestly replied, "I can't explain it. I basically haven't done anything different other than to try to hit the ball hard. Before, I would hit a sacrifice fly with the bases loaded. Now, I think of hitting the ball hard. Consequently, if I get the ball in the air, it carries."

# REGGIE JACKSON:
# KING OF THE WHIFFERS

As far as strikeouts are concerned, Bobby Bonds of the San Francisco Giants established the single season record in 1970 when he whiffed 189 times. Despite that horrendous whiff total, Bonds still managed to bat .302 and score 134 runs.

Bonds' whiff record may not stand up much longer, however, under the "onslaught" of today's free-swinging power hitters. Bo Jackson, for one, was well on his way toward a 200-plus strikeout season with the Kansas City Royals in 1987, when he was benched for a long period, which happens when you don't get hits.

Babe Ruth for years held the all-time career strikeout record of 1,330, but in recent years many players have surpassed that figure. By the time Reggie Jackson, the all-time leading whiffer, retired after the 1987 season, he nearly *doubled* Ruth's total with more than 2,600 strikeouts.

# BASEBALLS TRAVEL LIKE ROCKETS—CAN EVEN SCARE VETERAN PLAYERS

Brooks Robinson, the Baltimore Orioles Hall of Fame third baseman, said at an All-Star Game several years ago in response to our question: "I can't recall my strangest moment in baseball but I remember the scariest.

"One summer afternoon in 1969 or 1970, we were playing the Washington Senators at Baltimore and big Frank Howard, who was at his peak, sent a vicious liner that whistled just a few inches over my head. I didn't even have time to react to that drive, and within a split second I heard the ball strike the base of the bleacher wall some 370 feet away! If the ball had hit me full force, I might well have been decapitated. From that point on I played Howard deep, really deep . . . and I knew he would never call my bluff and bunt for a base hit."

Some time after the Robinson interview, we got hold of Frank Howard, a 6-foot-7-inch 265-pound giant of a man who looks like an overloaded truck, and asked him if any of his drives ever knocked down an infielder. (Howard batted righthanded.)

"Not that I recall," answered Howard, one of baseball's most amiable men and now a Milwaukee Brewers coach, but I did notice that almost all third basemen played me in the outfield grass."

Brooks Robinson is not unusual in being scared of line drives. Players who have been injured by jetlike drives have reason to be fearful.

Mark Eichhorn, the top Toronto Blue Jays' righthanded relief pitcher, working on the mound in the eighth inning of a Saturday afternoon, September 19th game (in New York's Yankee Stadium) threw a fastball to Yankees' outfielder Claudell Washington, who drilled a scorching line drive right back at Eichhorn.

Eichhorn instinctively moved his glove up to his lower chest in self-protection and luckily caught the ball. It was hit so hard that his left gloved hand was driven smack into his body and he was very nearly toppled over backward, but he still managed to hang onto the spheroid.

The Blue Jays trainer rushed out of the dugout to examine Eichhorn to see if there were any broken ribs or other injuries, but the big 6-foot-3-inch 210-pound pitcher said he was okay and just needed a couple of minutes to pull himself back together again.

If a pitcher doesn't react quickly enough, a direct hit from a wicked line drive can cause serious injury, as would be expected. For example, Cleveland's ace lefthander Herb Score, in May 1957, sustained a severe eye injury when struck by a bullet line drive from New York Yankee shortstop Gil McDougald's bat. Mr. Score was washed up for the season and failed in several subsequent comeback attempts to regain his old form.

In the 1937 All-Star Game played at Washington's Griffith Stadium, St. Louis Cardinal ace Dizzy Dean tried to log a fastball past Cleveland's Earl Averill. A good fastball hitter, Averill rifled a savage liner back to the box. The ball struck Dean on the left foot and bounded away. Dean chased it down and nipped Averill at first on a close play, but when he reached the clubhouse he discovered his big toe was broken.

The play proved to be the turning point in Dean's career. He began pitching again long before the injury healed completely, and in doing so he was forced to change his motion. That placed an unnatural strain on his right arm and shoulder and he lost his great speed.

Dean hung on in the majors for several more years, but his glory days were over as he had to rely on guile rather than speed in trying to retire batters.

Talking of players of an earlier era who could hit baseballs like rockets, Fred Lindstrom, the New York Giants star third baseman-outfielder of the 1920–30s and a Hall of Famer, told us, at a 1978 Shea Stadium old-timers game:

"When Rogers Hornsby was winning all those batting championships with the St. Louis Cardinals in the 1920s, he could hit a ball harder than anyone I saw. He batted righthanded, as you know, and all the infielders, including the second baseman, played him back on the grass . . . and many times I saw a Hornsby drive almost literally tear a fielder's glove off his hand. Lot of times, for example, the third baseman was just able to knock down a Hornsby shot, but the official scorers usually ruled a base hit because the ball was just 'too hot to handle.'"

How fast do line drives travel?

Top speed measured for any ball thrown by a pitcher is 100.9 miles per hour (Nolan Ryan, 1974), while a batted ball of the Claudell Washington line-drive variety under discussion here travels at least 150 miles per hour!

If a line drive travels 150 miles an hour through the pitcher's box, the Frank Howard liner over third base that scared Brooks Robinson could well have traveled 140 miles an hour plus.

# 6. THE STRANGE DH RULE

## PITCHER WAS SUCH A TERRIBLE BATTER HE BROUGHT ON THE DH RULE

Al Benton is best known in baseball trivia circles as the only major league pitcher to have faced both Babe Ruth (1934) and Mickey Mantle (1952) in regular season games, but he should be better known for his poor hitting. Benton, a big 6-foot-4-inch 220-pound righthander, broke into the big leagues with the Philadelphia Athletics in 1934 at the age of 23.

In compiling a 7-9 season record, Benton faced the Yankees and Babe Ruth several times during the course of the 1934 campaign, Ruth's final year in the American League. (Ruth did play in 28 games for the National League's Boston Braves in 1935 before retiring.)

Benton played the 1935 season with the Athletics, and then spent the next two years in the minors before re-emerging in the majors with the Detroit Tigers in 1938. He remained with the Tigers through 1948, with a break while he served in the U.S. military during the height of World War II in 1943–44.

He saw action on the mound for the Cleveland Indians in 1949–50 and was shipped down to the minors for all of 1951, but the intrepid Benton came up with the Boston Red Sox in 1952 for his final year in the big leagues as a relief specialist, compiling a 4-3 record in 24 games. It was in 1952 that the 41-year-old Benton faced Mickey Mantle, then the new home run phenom, who had established himself as a star in his sophomore year with the New York Yankees.

Benton was a good journeyman pitcher, going 98–88 lifetime, together with posting a respectable 3.66 ERA, but his hitting was what should not be forgotten. It was moundsmen like Benton who helped make the Designated Hitter rule an eventual reality in the major leagues, or at least in the American League. He was a shining example of pitchers who were such ludicrous hitters that they actually spoiled the look of the game.

Remember that Al Benton was a big man, as big and powerful a potential home run hitter as Hank Greenberg and Mark McGwire, but he stood at the plate like a wooden Indian, and usually took nothing more than halfhearted swings at pitched balls.

In his 14-year big league career, Benton batted 512 times, and managed to "eke out" 50 base hits for a horrendous .098 average. He hit exactly 7 doubles, no triples and no homers (for a .111 "slugging" average), scored 22 runs, and batted in 14. He walked only 7 times, but struck out an even 200 times.

And for all those sad batting stats, Benton was not even baseball's poorest hitting pitcher—a few others (including Bob Buhl) had even worse records, strangely enough.

In all fairness, however, we cannot blame the pitchers entirely for this sordid state of affairs, since managers often told them, especially on hot, humid days, just to walk up to the plate, take three strikes, and sit down as quickly as possible so as not to waste energy running the bases.

# FIRST (ILLEGAL) USE OF A DESIGNATED HITTER

There were mutterings for a DH rule as far back as the 1930s. Hitting was the dominant factor in baseball in the 1930s and 8 batters out of 9 got the job done, so the DH idea failed to take hold. Then much later, pitchers began to rule the game and scores were low, so the pitcher's turn at bat became more important.

Interestingly, several informal and abortive attempts at using a DH were made many years before the rule was officially adopted by the American League in 1973. For example, a little known exception was made in 1939 when Chicago White Sox pitcher Bill "Bullfrog" Dietrich found himself struggling during the course of a hot midsummer afternoon against the Cleveland Indians at Comiskey Park, Chicago. Sox manager Jimmy Dykes went over to Cleveland manager Oscar Vitt and asked him if it was all right with Vitt if Dykes used a pinch hitter for Dietrich but allowed Bullfrog to remain in the game. "It's okay with me if it's okay with the umpires," said the gentlemanly Vitt.

The pinch hitter was used and Dietrich remained in the game!

## BOB BUHL GOES 0 FOR 70

In respect to all-time weak-hitting pitchers, Bob Buhl rates a top spot in that category. While with the Chicago Cubs and Milwaukee Braves in 1962, Buhl "distinguished" himself by going 0 for 70, winding up with a batting average of .000. No other player in major league history, pitcher or otherwise, has gone to bat that many times in a season without a single bingle.

Buhl struck out about half the time; 36 K's were registered against him during that ignominious 0 for 70 streak at bat, though he did manage to walk six times, and score two runs.

Over the course of 15 years in the big leagues (1953–67), Buhl went 76 for 857, good for an .089 average, and somehow he managed two doubles which brought his "slugging" average up to .091. He scored a grand total of 31 runs, drove in 26 and struck out 389 times.

As a pitcher, however, Buhl posted a very competent 166-132 for a .557 percentage, reaching his peak in 1957 for Milwaukee when he went 18-7 as he played a key role in helping the Braves capture the National League pennant. Bob Buhl's record as a batsman literally cried out for the DH rule.

# RELIEF PITCHERS NEED
# RELIEF AT BAT

Batting records for relief pitchers are also quite awful. Hank Aguirre, a 6-foot-4-inch 210-pound lefthander, who spent the majority of his career as a reliever, is renowned in baseball history for being an unusually weak hitter—and he had plenty of time to roll up a horrendous batting record since his pitching skills kept him in the majors for 16 years (1955–70).

In 447 games, Aguirre came to the plate 388 times and managed to get exactly 33 hits, good for an .085 average. He rapped out seven doubles and one triple, giving him a .108 "slugging" average, scored 14 runs and drove in 21. He struck out 237 times, or about 60 percent of the time he came to bat.

Though Aguirre threw lefthanded, he batted righthanded for the first decade of his major league career, and then in 1965 he decided to become a switch-hitter—but his average still remained in the lower depths.

Aguirre's lifetime pitching log is something not to be sneezed at as he posted a 75-72 won-lost record with 33 saves and a low ERA of 3.24.

Wes Stock was a highly reliable righthanded relief pitcher for the Baltimore Orioles and Kansas City Athletics in the American League for nine years (1959–67), as he won 27, lost 13, saved 22, and fashioned a 3.60 ERA.

Stock's hitting was something else. A big 6-foot-2-inch 195-pounder, he waved a very weak stick as he banged out exactly 3 singles in 59 times at bat, good for an .051 batting average. Since he had no extra-base hits, the "slugging" average also came out to a cool .051. Stock had trouble making contact as he struck out 37 times, or approximately 2 out of every 3 at-bats.

Bob Feller may have been one of the greatest pitchers of all time but as a hitter he adopted a batting stance so unusual that he looked like a pretzel twisted out of shape. Miraculously, he still managed to bat .151 lifetime.

We recall a big league game we saw at Boston's Fenway Park in the mid-1950s when a small boy of 8 or 9 asked his father: "Daddy, why does that man bat so funny?"

"Well," came the answer, "he's not supposed to be much of a batter, son, he's the pitcher."

Even kids are appalled at pitchers in the National League flailing away in the batter's box struggling to get base hits. Kids often can do better.

Vernon "Lefty" Gomez, the great New York Yankees moundsman, was such a terrible hitter that he joked about it constantly. When he had a triple by-pass heart operation in the mid-1970s, Gomez remarked to a reporter: "That's the first triple I've had in my life." Gomez spoke the truth because in 904 major league at-bats, he had 133 base hits, including 11 doubles, but no triples or homers, which amounted to a .147 average (.159 "slugging").

Ironically enough, Gomez drove in the first run in All-Star history with a timely base hit. In the bottom of the second inning of the inaugural game played at Chicago's Comiskey Park on July 6, 1933, Gomez, facing "Wild Bill" Hallahan, lined a hard single to centerfield scoring Jimmy Dykes from second base.

"That's why baseball is so interesting . . . the unexpected can happen anytime," said Gomez recently.

# STILL A REGULAR AT 44—
# YAZ SETS MARK FOR
# LONG CAREER

Carl Yastrzemski starred for the Boston Red Sox for 23 years, and in 1983, at the age of 44, he became the oldest player in modern big league history to play regularly. Though "Yaz" was an outfielder for most of his career he saw service mostly as a designated hitter in 1983—his final season—as he played in 119 games, collected 101 base hits and batted a respectable .266.

In sporting the Red Sox uniform for nearly a quarter-century, Yastrzemski set an American League record by playing in the most games—3,308—and registering the most times at bat—11,988—while slamming out 3,419 base hits,

The last swing of a 44-year-old—Yaz.

(Photo—Steve Babineau)

good for a solid .285 lifetime batting average. He also won three batting championships (including a "Triple Crown" in 1967 when he swatted .326, bashed 44 homers and drove in 121 runs). He also tied a major league record by playing in 100 or more games for 22 seasons, and led the American League in intentional walks—190.

He is certain to be elected into baseball's Hall of Fame at Cooperstown in 1989, his first year of eligibility.

Carl Yastrzemski's endurance records were subsequently tied and/or broken by Pete Rose of the Cincinnati Reds. In 1985, the 44-year-old Rose, by then the Reds manager, played in 119 games (mostly at first base), tying Yaz, and in 1986, at the age of 45, he played semi-regularly (72 games) at first before he benched himself permanently (as it turned out) in mid-August.

# EXTEND THE DH RULE TO BOTH LEAGUES

Because of the lack of hitting, fan interest began declining seriously and baseball executives came to the conclusion that pitchers in particular exacerbated the situation by being chronic "out men" and should have their bats taken away.

Thus, the idea of the Designated Hitter rule took firm hold and trials were held in the minor leagues before it was introduced in the American League in 1973. When you get down to it there's something really strange about the DH rule. Each side has 10 men, but only 9 bat. The pitcher sticks to his pitching and doesn't embarrass himself as a batter.

The National League in not adopting the DH rule, unfortunately, has not yet seen the light of day.

Over a generation ago, the moguls of professional football refined the game by dividing teams into separate offensive and defensive units, and allowing unlimited substitution. A quarterback, for example, never plays as a defensive back, or a fullback operating as a linebacker. They used to—but no more. The "two-way" football player has gone the way of the carrier pigeon, and there's no question that specialization has helped football tremendously.

By comparison, the American League thus far has instituted a relatively minor change in relieving the pitcher of his hitting responsibilities.

In the World Series the National League has a decided edge because in those games played in the home park of the NL team, the AL pitcher has to bat. Since, during the whole year every year the AL pitcher hasn't wielded a bat and is now called on to hit the ball, the ninth spot in the batting order is almost always an automatic out for the AL team. Besides, since no DH bats in the NL park, that leaves the AL with one batter short. Actually, the AL is thus two batters weaker—no DH and a weak-hitting pitcher.

Then in the American League park, the NL gets the advantage of having a strong batter replacing a probably weak-hitting hurler at bat. Not fair!

All-Star Games without the DH are likewise unfair to the AL.

Harsh critics of the Designated Hitter rule like the late Dick Young of the *New York Post* and Bart Giamatti, National League president, say that the use of the DH lessens the number of strategic moves a manager can make during the course of the game. That may be so, but there's still nothing stranger than seeing an excellent pitcher flailing away in frustration trying to hit a baseball.

# 7. WEAK HITTERS AND BIG LOSERS

## SCOTT SETS CONSECUTIVE GAME RECORD BEFORE BEING BENCHED FOR WEAK HITTING

Everett "Deacon" Scott, a native of Bluffton, Indiana, broke into the major leagues in 1914 with the Boston Red Sox as a 21-year-old shortstop, and just over two years later, on June 20, 1916, began one of the most remarkable streaks in baseball history. From that day through the 1921 season he never missed a game with the Red Sox—over 800 of them.

After the 1921 campaign, Scott went to the New York Yankees in a multi-player trade, and from that point continued his "Iron Man" role. A fine fielder, he went more than three additional seasons, never missing being in the lineup through May 5, 1925. This ran his streak of consecutive games played to 1,307. Scott, a runt of a man standing 5 feet 8 inches and weighing 150 pounds, but an extremely durable athlete, became the first man in professional baseball to play more than 1,000 games in a row.

Scott could have gone on to extend his streak even further but Yankees manager Miller Huggins had to bench him for weak hitting! The Yankees in those years with Babe Ruth were called "Murderers' Row" and Scott batted around .250.

Interestingly, Scott's teammate, the hard-hitting, 22-year-old first baseman named Lou Gehrig began his own record-breaking streak of 2,130 straight games on June 1, 1925, less than a month after the Little Deacon was benched.

In early August 1925, Scott was sent to the Washington Senators on waivers and finished his big league career with the Chicago White Sox and Cincinnati Reds in 1926.

Everett Scott ended with a career batting average of a modest .249 in 1,654 major league games, but had remained in the lineup on a daily basis so long because of his surehanded fielding. He led American League shortstops in fielding percentage for a record eight years, all in succession, 1916 through 1923.

# DEL ENNIS LEAVES 500 STRANDED—CLEAN-UP HITTER CAN'T CLEAN UP

Del Ennis, a hard-hitting outfielder, came up with the Philadelphia Phillies in 1946 and reached his peak in 1950 when he helped the Phillies' so-called "Whiz Kids" to the National League pennant. Ennis compiled excellent stats that year—he hit 31 homers, drove in a league high 126 runs, and averaged .311 at bat.

However, a team of sportswriters for the *Philadelphia Inquirer* still felt that Ennis, hitting in the fourth position, wasn't driving in enough runs, particularly since the three batters who ordinarily preceded him in the order (Eddie Waitkus, Richie Ashburn and Willie "Puddin' Head" Jones) always seemed to be on base. The reporters went back and checked the results of every game and discovered that Ennis left over 500 men on base during the course of the 1950 season.

"If that isn't a record for leaving men on, it sure comes close to it!" one of the writers declared. "If Ennis was a better clutch hitter—and with all those men he had on base—he could have easily broken Hack Wilson's major league record of 190 runs batted in for one season."

The Phillies experienced total disaster in the World Series that year as they were wiped out by the Yankees in four straight games. Ennis didn't help the cause much as he went 2 for 14 and failed to drive in a single run.

# BATTING AVERAGES HIT BOTTOM—ONLY ONE .300 HITTER IN A.L.

By the middle 1960s hitting in the majors, especially in the American League, had declined so much that the lords of baseball decided something had to be done. The low point for hitting came in 1968 when the ten American League teams posted a combined batting average of .230. The Minnesota Twins took the team batting crown with a "robust" .240, while the New York Yankees finished last with an anemic .214 mark. Carl Yastrzemski of the Boston Red Sox had the distinction of being the A.L.'s only .300 hitter, taking the batting crown with a .301 average, the lowest average for a batting leader in major league history.

The National League did a bit better as their ten teams combined for a .243 batting mark.

By contrast, in 1930, considered to be the peak year for major league hitting, the eight American League teams posted a combined .288 mark, while the eight National League clubs swatted .303. The New York Giants led the parade with a very substantial .319 team average.

# SENATORS, WITH WALTER JOHNSON, BIG LOSERS BUT NOT THE WORST

The Washington Senators experienced their worst season in 1909 as they finished dead last under manager Joe Cantillon with a 42-110 record, for a lowly .276 percentage. The Senators wound up exactly 56 games behind the pennant-winning Detroit Tigers.

The Senators started the season badly, but sagged even more in midseason. Of the 34 games played in July, they managed to lose 29. That still remains as the all-time record for the most games lost by one team in a month.

For the season, the great Walter Johnson, then in his third year in the majors, rolled up a dismal 13-25 won-lost record, while his fellow righthander, rookie Bob Groom, "fashioned" a 7-26 mark. No big league pitcher in the 20th century has lost more games in a season than Bob Groom.

Though they were big losers, Johnson and Groom could justifiably complain about weak hitting support since they posted glittering earned run averages of 2.21 and 2.87, respectively. In team batting Washington finished last with a puny .223 mark.

Was this baseball's "worst" team? No. Other teams have actually experienced worse months. In August 1890, the National League Pittsburgh Pirates went 1-27, and the Cleveland Spiders tied that record in their final National League year in 1899, when they staggered to a 1-27 record for the month of September.

Pittsburgh for the entire 1890 season wound up with a miserable 23-113 (.169 percentage), while the 1899 Cleveland Spiders finished with a horrendous 20-134 record (.149 percentage). No other major league team has surpassed this.

# STRANGE DEMISE OF THE METS . . . A LITTLE BIRD DID THEM IN

The New York Mets in 1986 dominated baseball as they posted a glittering 108-54 won-lost mark in finishing first in the National League's Eastern Division 21½ games ahead of the second-place Philadelphia Phillies. The Mets went on to defeat the Houston Astros, the N.L.'s Western Division Champs, four games to two in the League Championship Series, and climaxed their amazing season by whipping the Boston Red Sox four games to three in a dramatic World Series. The Mets reigned supreme as baseball's World Champions.

The 1987 New York Mets never seemed to get off on the right foot as they went on to disappoint their fans by finishing second in the N.L. East, five games behind the St. Louis Cardinals. All sorts of strange happenings prevented the Mets from reaching the top for a second straight season.

For starters, Ray Knight, their star third baseman and World Series MVP, defected to the Baltimore Orioles after a contract dispute, and Dwight Gooden, their top pitcher, spent the first two months in a drug rehab clinic. Several other key pitchers, including Bob Ojeda and Rick Aguilera, were out for long spells with injuries.

However, the strangest incident of all that may have typified the Mets' ill luck in 1987 occurred at the Sunday, April 12 game at Shea Stadium when the '86 champs faced the Atlanta Braves. Dion James, Braves outfielder, hit a fly ball toward left centerfield, but before any Met could catch up to it, the ball struck and killed a pigeon in full flight. Both the ball and pigeon dropped down onto the field in a thud and James was awarded a ground rule double. The Mets went on to lose that game 11-4.

When Rafael Santana, Mets shortstop, picked up the dead bird in his hand, he muttered, "We're not getting any breaks at all."

Rafael Santana
is kind to birdies.

(Photo—Michael Ponzini)

# 8. RECORD GAMES

## GRIMES REMEMBERS GAME WHEN HE MADE 8 OUTS IN 4 AT-BATS

Burleigh Grimes, a fiercely competitive spitball-tossing righthander, whose 270-212 record compiled over 19 big league seasons (1916–34) earned him election to the Hall of Fame in 1964, often liked to recall decades-old events in his career. His favorite spot as a raconteur was the lobby of the grand old Hotel Otesaga in Cooperstown, but whenever the 1920 World Series matching the Cleveland Indians against his Brooklyn Dodgers was mentioned, his mood turned dark.

"I never did like that 1920 World Series," Grimes snorted, eyes flashing, during an Otesaga interview little more than two years before his death on December 6, 1985, at the age of 92.

"Why not?" we asked, knowing, of course, that the Indians whipped the Dodgers five games to two. (After 1921, the World Series was placed on a best out of seven basis.)

"Because three or four of our key players violated curfew and didn't show up at the park in the best of shape to play ball!" Grimes snapped. Naturally, he didn't want to name names, and closed that part of the conversation by declaring, "Let 'em rest in peace!"

What particularly struck us was that Grimes got so emotional about a series of games played more than 60 years ago. He spoke as if they were played yesterday!

Grimes ranked as the ace of the Brooklyn pitching staff in 1920, posting a 23-11 record and leading the National League in winning percentage with .676. (This was the first of his five 20-victory seasons in the big leagues and the first of his four World Series.)

Grimes started three games in the Series, winning one, the second game (played at Brooklyn), and losing the fifth and seventh games played in Cleveland's League Park.

That fifth game, staged on Sunday, October 10, turned out to be one of the strangest and most memorable in World Series history. Grimes got belted around as he gave up 9 hits and 7 runs in $3\frac{1}{3}$ innings. Four of those runs came in the first inning as rightfielder Elmer Smith, a left-handed hitter, bashed a bases-loaded homer over the high rightfield wall, the first World Series grand-slammer.

"I threw Smith a low fastball and apparently that's the kind of pitch he liked because he really jumped on it," grumbled Grimes. "The scouting report we got on Smith was no good . . . . I should have pitched him high and tight," Grimes added.

Clarence Mitchell, the lefthander who relieved Grimes in the fourth inning, gave the game further historic dimensions when he lined into a triple play in the fifth.

With Pete Kilduff on second and Otto Miller on first, and on the move, pitcher Mitchell hit a sharp liner at second baseman Bill Wambsganss (usually shortened to Wamby). Wamby, who was running over to cover his bag, grabbed the ball in midair, stepped on second base before Kilduff could get back, and then wheeled around and tagged Miller, who was running down from first. This was the only *unassisted* triple play in World Series history. Cleveland took this game by an 8-1 count.

"Sure, Wamby made a good play, but you've got to admit he had more luck than brains in making this kind of unassisted triple play," growled Grimes.

Incidentally, Mitchell had the unfortunate experience of hitting into five putouts in two times at bat that day, since in the eighth inning he grounded into a double play! Mitchell was considered a good-hitting pitcher and was occasionally used at first base and in the outfield.

"Burleigh Grimes had no one to blame but himself when the Chicago Cubs beat him 3 to 2 in 12 innings, extending the losing streak of the visitors to 9 games," said *The Sporting News* in its account of a Cubs–Brooklyn Dodgers game played at Wrigley Field on September 22, 1925.

TSN didn't take Grimes to task for his pitching—he only gave up 3 runs in 12 innings—but for his batting! *TSN*

## BOX SCORE
### World Series Fifth Game
### Sunday, Oct. 10, 1920—At Cleveland

| Brooklyn | AB | R | H | PO | A | Cleveland | AB | R | H | PO | A |
|----------|----|----|----|----|----|-----------|----|----|----|----|----|
| Olson, ss ... | 4 | 0 | 2 | 3 | 5 | Jamieson, lf . | 4 | 1 | 2 | 2 | 1 |
| Sheehan, 3b. | 4 | 0 | 1 | 1 | 1 | (a)Graney, lf . | 1 | 0 | 0 | 0 | 0 |
| Griffith, rf .. | 4 | 0 | 0 | 0 | 0 | Wamby, 2b .. | 5 | 1 | 1 | 7 | 2 |
| Wheat, lf ... | 4 | 1 | 2 | 3 | 0 | Speaker, cf .. | 3 | 2 | 1 | 1 | 0 |
| Myers, cf ... | 4 | 0 | 2 | 0 | 0 | Smith, rf ... | 4 | 1 | 3 | 0 | 0 |
| Konetchy, 1b. | 4 | 0 | 2 | 9 | 2 | Gardner, 3b . | 4 | 0 | 1 | 2 | 2 |
| Kilduff, 2b .. | 4 | 0 | 1 | 5 | 6 | Johnston, 1b. | 3 | 1 | 2 | 9 | 1 |
| Miller, c .... | 2 | 0 | 2 | 0 | 1 | Sewell, ss ... | 3 | 0 | 0 | 2 | 4 |
| Krueger, c .. | 2 | 0 | 1 | 2 | 1 | O'Neill, c ... | 2 | 1 | 0 | 3 | 1 |
| Grimes, p ... | 1 | 0 | 0 | 0 | 1 | Thomas, c .. | 0 | 0 | 0 | 1 | 0 |
| Mitchell, p .. | 2 | 0 | 0 | 1 | 0 | Bagby, p .... | 4 | 1 | 2 | 0 | 2 |
| Totals ...... | 34 | 1 | 13 | 24 | 17 | Totals ...... | 33 | 8 | 12 | 27 | 12 |

(a) Struck out for Jamieson in eighth.

| | | | | | | | | | |
|---|---|---|---|---|---|---|---|---|---|
| Brooklyn ........ | 0 0 0 | 0 0 0 | 0 0 1—1 |
| Cleveland ....... | 4 0 0 | 3 1 0 | 0 0 x—8 |

Errors—Sheehan, Gardner, O'Neill. Runs batted in—Smith 4, Bagby 3, Gardner, Konetchy. Three-base hits—Konetchy, Smith. Home runs—Smith, Bagby. Sacrifices—Sheehan, Johnston. Double plays—Olson, Kilduff and Konetchy; Jamieson and O'Neill; Gardner, Wamby and Johnston; Johnston, Sewell and Johnston. Triple play—Wamby unassisted. Left on bases—Brooklyn 7, Cleveland 6. Passed ball—Miller. Umpires—Klem (N.L.), Connolly (A.L.), O'Day (N.L.), and Dinneen (A.L.). Time—1:49. Attendance—26,884.

### Pitching Summary

| | IP | H | BB | SO | HB | WP |
|---|----|----|----|----|----|----|
| Grimes (L) .... | 3 1/3 | 9 | 1 | 0 | 0 | 0 |
| Mitchell ....... | 4 2/3 | 3 | 3 | 1 | 0 | 0 |
| Bagby (W) ..... | 9 | 13 | 0 | 3 | 0 | 1 |

pointed out: "Grimes had the distinction of hitting into two double plays and a triple play . . . on each occasion he blasted promising rallies."

In his other trip to the plate, "Lord Burleigh," as he was known in Brooklyn, struck out—thus, he made 8 outs in 4 at-bats, not an easy task to accomplish.

In Grimes' defense, let us note that the two double plays and the triple play came as the result of hard-hit grounders. In the triple play, which came in the eighth inning with the Dodgers' Chuck Corgan on third and Zack Taylor on first, Grimes sent a sizzling grounder down to Sparky Adams at shortstop. Adams flipped the ball to second baseman Gale Staley forcing Taylor, and Staley's relay to first baseman Charlie Grimm doubled Grimes. Corgan attempted to score on the play, but was nipped out at the plate on Grimm's rifle throw to catcher Gabby Hartnett.

(Oddly enough, Staley played in exactly seven major league games in his career, all with the Cubs in September 1925, and within that short span participated in a triple play. Many major leaguers having lengthy careers never see a triple play.)

In 1983, just as he was turning 90, Grimes still remembered that unusual September, 1925 game against the Cubs and made these comments: "I hit the ball hard three times that day, but they all went straight at someone— that's baseball. And remember, I was considered as a pretty good hitting pitcher."

The record books bear Grimes out for he hit a respectable .248 lifetime, didn't strike out too much, and was used occasionally as a pinch hitter.

# IN HEAVIEST SCORING GAME, 26-23, CUBS ALMOST BLOW 26-9 LEAD IN 7TH!

So ran the evening headline on Tuesday, August 25, 1922, after a perfect afternoon for baseball at Chicago's Wrigley Field. The players had taken their positions on the field promptly at 3:00 P.M. under an azure sky with the temperature in the low 70s.

The Cubs-Phillies match-up had no special significance since at this late date in the season both teams were for all intents and purposes well out of the National League pennant race, but after the last putout was made 3 hours and one minute later—at precisely 6:01 P.M.—the game had earned its place in the annals of diamond lore, as 49 runners had crossed the plate with the Cubs pounding out a 26-23 victory, making this the highest scoring major league game in history.

And when we speak about "major league history" here, we go back to the time when the National League was founded in 1876, and do not refer to the so-called post-1900 "modern era." Moreover, the 51 total base hits, 26 by Philadelphia and 25 by Chicago, still stands as another all-time record.

This hectic slugging match began in a mild enough manner as the Phillies failed to score in the first inning off Cubs' righthander Tony Kaufmann, while the Cubs managed to touch Phils righty Jimmy Ring for a single tally in the bottom half of the opening frame. Things did begin heating up in the second inning as the Phillies pushed three runs across the plate while the Cubs unloaded on Ring for ten runs. Phillies manager Irv "Kaiser" Wilhelm permitted Ring to endure that unmerciful shelling and hardly gave a thought to signaling the bullpen for a relief pitcher. (Wilhelm knew what it was to suffer indignities as a pitcher for as a member of the Boston Braves staff in 1905, he had compiled an unenviable 4-22 record.)

In the third inning, the Phils chipped away at Kaufmann for two more scores, while Ring, who apparently had regained his composure, blanked the Cubs.

The Phils added another run in the top of the fourth to bring the score to a more respectable 11-6, but in the Cubs' half of the inning they really got their heavy artillery going by scoring 14 runs, tying the record for most runs by one team in a single inning (since broken). With only one out and 6 runs already across in that disastrous inning Manager Wilhelm had pulled Ring out of there in favor of Phil "Lefty" Weinert, who continued to absorb the punishment.

A total of 19 men came to the plate for the Cubs in the fourth, with outfielder Marty Callaghan equaling a major league record by batting three times in a single inning—he singled twice and struck out once.

When the dust cleared, Weinert finally settled down and permitted only one more run, that one in the sixth, bringing the score to 26-9. (The Phils had picked up three more in the fifth.)

The Phillies appeared to have been blown completely out of the game, but after they were held at bay in the sixth and seventh they went to work against a series of Cubs relievers in the eighth and ninth innings as they scored 14 times: 8 in the eighth and 6 in the ninth, running the final score to 26-23. Reliever Ernie Osborne got the last Phillie out in the 9th with the bases loaded!

"The Phillies tried to put a scare into us, but as far as we're concerned, the game's outcome was never really in doubt," Cubs manager Bill Killifer remarked later.

Though he only pitched four innings, Tony Kaufmann was declared the winning hurler (scoring rules were a bit different in those days).

Hitting stars for the Cubs included Cliff Heathcote who went 5 for 5, and Hack Miller and Marty Krug who each had four hits. Among Miller's double brace of hits were two homers. Charlie Hollocher contributed a double and two singles.

Leading the slugging parade for the Phils were Russ Wrightstone and Curt Walker who slammed out four hits each, and Bevo LeBourveau, Johnny Mokan and Cliff Lee who each chipped in with three.

This wild and woolly game was also marked by 20 bases on balls (each team giving up 10) and 10 errors, with the Cubs and Phils committing 5 each.

## BOX SCORE

| Philadelphia | AB | R | H | PO | A | | Chicago | AB | R | H | PO | A |
|---|---|---|---|---|---|---|---|---|---|---|---|---|
| Wrightstone, 3b. | 7 | 3 | 4 | 0 | 1 | | Heathcote, cf. | 5 | 5 | 5 | 4 | 0 |
| Parkinson, 2b . . | 4 | 1 | 2 | 4 | 6 | | Hollocher, ss . | 5 | 2 | 3 | 5 | 2 |
| Williams, cf . . . | 3 | 1 | 0 | 2 | 0 | | Kelleher, ss . . | 1 | 0 | 0 | 0 | 0 |
| LeBourveau, cf. | 4 | 2 | 3 | 0 | 0 | | Terry, 2b . . . . | 5 | 2 | 2 | 2 | 2 |
| Walker, rf . . . . . | 6 | 2 | 4 | 2 | 0 | | Friberg, 2b . . | 1 | 0 | 1 | 0 | 0 |
| Mokan, lf . . . . . | 4 | 2 | 3 | 1 | 0 | | Grimes, 1b . . | 4 | 2 | 2 | 7 | 1 |
| Fletcher, ss . . . . | 3 | 1 | 0 | 0 | 2 | | Callaghan, rf. | 7 | 3 | 2 | 2 | 0 |
| J. Smith, ss . . . | 4 | 2 | 1 | 1 | 3 | | Miller, lf . . . . | 5 | 3 | 4 | 1 | 0 |
| Leslie, 1b . . . . . | 2 | 1 | 0 | 4 | 0 | | Krug, 3b . . . . | 5 | 4 | 4 | 1 | 1 |
| Lee, 1b . . . . . . . | 4 | 4 | 3 | 6 | 0 | | O'Farrell, c . . | 3 | 3 | 2 | 1 | 1 |
| Henline, c . . . . | 2 | 1 | 2 | 4 | 0 | | Hartnett, c . . | 0 | 0 | 0 | 4 | 0 |
| Withrow, c . . . . | 4 | 1 | 2 | 0 | 0 | | Kaufmann, p . . | 2 | 0 | 0 | 0 | 1 |
| Ring, p . . . . . . . | 2 | 0 | 1 | 0 | 1 | | (a) Barber . . . | 1 | 2 | 0 | 0 | 0 |
| Weinert, p . . . . | 4 | 2 | 1 | 0 | 0 | | Stueland, p . | 1 | 0 | 0 | 0 | 0 |
| (c) Rapp . . . . . . | 0 | 0 | 0 | 0 | 0 | | (b) Maisel . . . | 1 | 0 | 0 | 0 | 0 |
| Totals . . . . . . . . | 53 | 23 | 26 | 24 | 14 | | Eubanks, p . . | 0 | 0 | 0 | 0 | 1 |
| (a) Batted for Kaufmann in fourth. | | | | | | | Morris, p . . . | 0 | 0 | 0 | 0 | 0 |
| (b) Batted for Stueland in seventh. | | | | | | | Osborne, p . . | 0 | 0 | 0 | 0 | 0 |
| (c) Batted for Weinert in ninth. | | | | | | | Totals . . . . . . . | 46 | 26 | 25 | 27 | 9 |

```
Philadelphia . . . . . . . 0  3  2    1  3  0    0  8  6—23
Chicago  . . . . . . . . . . 1 10  0   14  0  1    0  0  x—26
```

### Pitching Summary

| | IP | H | BB | SO | HB | WP |
|---|---|---|---|---|---|---|
| Kaufmann (W) . . . . . | 4 | 9 | 2 | 0 | 0 | 0 |
| Stueland . . . . . . . . . . | 3 | 7 | 2 | 2 | 0 | 1 |
| Eubanks . . . . . . . . . . | 2/3 | 3 | 3 | 0 | 0 | 0 |
| Morris . . . . . . . . . . . | 1/3 | 4 | 1 | 1 | 0 | 0 |
| Osborne . . . . . . . . . . | 1 | 3 | 2 | 3 | 0 | 0 |
| Ring (L) . . . . . . . . . | 3 1/3 | 12 | 5 | 2 | 0 | 0 |
| Weinert . . . . . . . . . . . | 4 2/3 | 13 | 5 | 2 | 1 | 0 |

Errors—Wrightstone 2, Williams, Walker, Lee, Heathcote, Hollocher, Callaghan, Krug, Hartnett. Two-base hits—Terry, Krug 2, Mokan, Hollocher, Heathcote 2, Grimes, Withrow, Friberg, Parkinson, Walker. Three-base hits—Walker, Wrightstone. Home runs—Miller 2, O'Farrell. Sacrifices—Leslie, O'Farrell, Hollocher, Walker. Double plays—J. Smith, Parkinson and Lee 2; Wrightstone, Parkinson and Lee. Left on bases—Philadelphia 16, Chicago 9. Hit by pitcher—By Weinert (Grimes). Umpires—Hart and Rigler. Time—3:01.

113

What is truly amazing is that a Donnybrook of this magnitude required just 3 hours and one minute to play.

Roy Leslie, Phillies first baseman, was sent down to the minors at the end of the 1922 season and wound up with Salt Lake City of the Pacific Coast League for the 1923 campaign. On May 11 of that year Leslie had the distinction of playing in the *highest scoring Pacific Coast League game* of all time as Vernon, California thrashed Salt Lake City 35-11 at Salt Lake. Leslie tried to help the cause with a homer and single, but all to no avail as Vernon's Pete Schneider led his wrecking crew with 5 homers, a double and 14 runs batted in!

# BLUE JAYS SET NEW RECORD, HAMMER 10 HOMERS IN ONE GAME

"I don't think anyone threw well. It was an embarrassing baseball game . . . I'm not the only one embarrassed. Everybody in the clubhouse is embarrassed," moaned Baltimore Orioles' manager Cal Ripken, Sr., after his team was devastated 18-3 by the Toronto Blue Jays at Toronto's Exhibition Stadium on Monday September 14, 1987.

What made the game particularly embarrassing for the Orioles was Toronto's awesome display of home run power. The Blue Jays hammered out 10 "dingers," breaking the major league record of 8 in one game. (The New York Yankees of 1939 set that mark the first time when they blasted 8 roundtrippers against the Philadelphia A's. Six other teams equaled that figure, with the most recent being the Montreal Expos' 8-homer barrage against the Atlanta Braves on July 30, 1978).

Blue Jays' catcher Ernie Whitt began the home run parade when he led off the second inning with a shot into the rightfield bleachers. Whitt, a 6-foot-1-inch 200-pound lefthanded pull hitter, belted another solo homer in the fifth inning, and added a 3-run poke in the seventh. (A number of renowned home run hitters, including Hank Greenberg, never hit 3 in a single game.)

114

Leftfielder George Bell and third baseman Rance Mulliniks each contributed two homers to the onslaught. Centerfielder Lloyd Moseby hit one out of the park and his late-inning replacement, rookie Rob Ducey, also got into the act with a drive into the rightfield seats. Designated hitter Fred McGriff, also a rookie, made it an even 10.

Baltimore Mike Hart, a rookie centerfielder, saved face for the Orioles slightly when he hit for the circuit in the third inning, making it 11 homers for the two teams, tying the all-time single game record set by the Yankees with six, and the Detroit Tigers, five, in 1950.

# SHORTEST GAME IN PRO BALL—9 INNINGS IN 32 MINUTES!

The average nine-inning major league game today requires about 2 hours and 45 minutes to complete. However, a game can be played much faster as was proved by the Southern Association who conducted an experiment on September 19, 1910, to see just how fast. They proved that 32 minutes is all you really need.

In this 32-minute game, Mobile edged the home team Atlanta Crackers 2-1. With the score tied 1-1 in the first half of the ninth, Mobile pushed across the decisive run. Both teams hustled every minute of the way. Batters did not wait out the pitchers, but rather swung at every good pitch. There was only one walk; not a single player struck out; and Mobile even reeled off a triple play. Mobile made 6 hits against 4 for Atlanta. On the same afternoon, Chattanooga at Nashville in another Southern Association game, needed only 42 minutes to complete.

# MINOR LEAGUE RECORDS
# SURPASS MAJORS—EXCEPT
# ONE FOR TRIPLES
# IN A SEASON

All major league records but one have been exceeded in the minors. When J. Owen "Chief" Wilson, Pittsburgh outfielder, slammed out 36 triples in 1912, that was to become the only major league seasonal record never to be surpassed in the minors. Standing second on the all-time professional baseball list is Jack Cross who hit 32 three-baggers for London in the Class B Michigan-Ontario League in 1925.

# 9. OFF THE FIELD

## BASEBALL HALL OF FAME HOUSES STRANGE SPECIMENS OF THE GAME

"Be careful how you hold this," Peter P. Clark, Baseball Hall of Fame Museum Registrar warned us as he handed over an artifact he pulled out of a cabinet in his lower level museum office. We followed Clark's advice because this particular specimen of diamond game memorabilia turned out to be a Gillette razor blade taped onto a sheet of letter paper inscribed with a note testifying to the fact that this blue blade was used by Cy Young on September 9, 1953, during a visit to a friend's house in East Cuyahoga Falls, Ohio.

The Cy Young razor blade is among numerous items in the Hall of Fame Museum collection not ordinarily placed on display. A razor blade in a baseball museum? Strange.

But that's not all. After Peter Clark gingerly placed the Cy Young Gillette blade back into the cabinet, he hauled out a chunk of wood, measuring about 16 inches in length and some 6 inches thick. This solid-looking specimen of wood—more specifically red oak—was inscribed in pen as being the last block of wood cut with an axe by Cy Young, and dated November 8, 1954. Moreover, Cy Young, the 511-game winner, who spent his long retirement from baseball as a farmer in Newcomerstown, Ohio, autographed the chunk of oak soon after he chopped it. He was 87 at the time. (Young died on November 4, 1955, at the age of 88.)

"The Cy Young oak is a part of our permanent holdings, but one wonders what a collector would pay for it at public auction," mused Clark. "Almost any sort of artifact dealing with a Hall of Famer seems to have special appeal," he added.

Cy Young, the hard-throwing righthander is, of course, baseball's all-time winningest pitcher with those 511 victories being rolled up over 22 seasons from 1890 to 1911.

---

Another highly unusual gift came to the Hall of Fame shortly after Johnny Mize was elected to baseball's shrine in 1981. The gift consisted of a large bucketful of red clay soil from the school playground in Demorest, Georgia, where Mize first began playing on the diamond. The contributor was Demorest's school superintendent.

In a 15-year major league career (1936–53, with three years out for military service in World War II), Johnny Mize slammed out 359 homers and averaged .312, while playing successively for the St. Louis Cards, New York Giants and New York Yankees.

---

When Phil Linz, New York Yankees infielder, played a loud harmonica in the back of the team bus after a late season 1964 game, manager Yogi Berra became so infuriated when Linz wouldn't "stop the music" that an altercation resulted. The "harmonica incident" led to Berra's departure as Yankees' pilot at season's end. Yes, Peter Clark has the harmonica—encased in its original box, no less—in his cabinets and it's been personally signed by Linz himself!

---

Nelson Fox isn't a Hall of Famer yet, but many baseball experts feel he should eventually gain election to baseball's shrine. During a 19-year big league career (1947–65), mostly with the Chicago White Sox, Fox batted a potent .288, lined out 2,663 base hits, and scintillated as a smooth fielding second baseman. After his premature death in 1975, members of Fox's family contributed a batch of the infielder's mementos to the Hall of Fame Museum. These included an unopened pouch of "Nelson Fox's Favorite Chewing Tobacco." Fox was such an inveterate chewer that one of the major tobacco companies produced and marketed his own special brand of chaw.

---

A piece of terra cotta measuring about 2 inches across, about 1/2 inch thick, and shaped exactly like a tiny catcher's mitt, was sent to the Baseball Museum recently with an attached note reading: "This catcher's mitt was used by the wee people's baseball team in Ireland many centuries ago."

We don't know for sure whether or not the Irish leprechauns played baseball, but the tiny glove has been duly registered and numbered for exhibit purposes by Clark.

In regard to the leprechaun's "catcher's mitt," we should emphasize that one of the Hall of Fame's key exhibits, a worn, misshapen, homemade baseball, is surrounded by legend and mystery. This baseball had been discovered in 1934 in a dust-covered attic trunk in a farmhouse in Fly Creek, New York, a crossroads village about 3 miles from Cooperstown. The farmhouse had been owned by Abner Graves, a boyhood friend of Abner Doubleday, who later claimed that Doubleday had "invented" baseball in Cooperstown in 1839. The ball, now known as the "Doubleday Baseball," was purchased for $5 shortly after it was found by Stephen C. Clark, a wealthy Cooperstown businessman, who founded the Baseball Hall of Fame and Museum in the late 1930s.

It was an 87-year-old Abner Graves who convinced the Mills Commission of 1906–07 (the Mills Commission was formed by the two major leagues to probe the origins of baseball) that he was with Doubleday in 1839 when baseball had its birth. And when that ball, purportedly used in one of those early ball games at Cooperstown, was found at Fly Creek, the village's locale as the birthplace of the diamond game was further corroborated. However, these conclusions are still hotly disputed. Among other things, Abner Doubleday was a cadet at the U.S. Military Academy at West Point in 1839 and did not even set foot in Cooperstown at the time.

Nevertheless, without Stephen C. Clark, we would not have a National Baseball Hall of Fame and Museum as we know it today.

The so-called "Doubleday Baseball" is conspicuously displayed near the Hall of Fame Museum's main entrance.

"Let me go. PLEASE let me go!"

# DRYSDALE ALMOST FAILED
# TO MAKE IT TO HIS
# HALL OF FAME INDUCTION

In the Hall of Fame's first half-century of existence just over
200 players, managers, umpires and executives have been
voted into baseball's shrine. A player must wait at least five
years after his retirement from the game before he is eligi-
ble to be voted upon, and sometimes, unfortunately, a diamond star is elected to the Hall of Fame long after he's
gone to the Great Beyond.

In the case of Don Drysdale, the righthanded power
pitcher of the old Dodgers from Brooklyn had to endure
a waiting period of 15 years before he was elected to the
Hall of Fame in 1984. Happily enough, he was very much
alive and well when he finally received the call, but he
almost missed out.

"Big D," as he was popularly known, posted a 209-166

won-lost record with the Brooklyn-Los Angeles Dodgers over a 14-year period (1956–69), and achieved one of baseball's truly noteworthy records in 1968 when he racked up six straight shutouts while hurling 58 consecutive scoreless innings.

"Election into Baseball's Hall of Fame is the highest tribute an athlete can ever receive." That is not just the opinion of Edward W. Stack, Hall of Fame President, but of thousands of fans as well.

Hall of Fame Induction Ceremonies are always elaborately staged gigantic media events with the newly minted enshrined being called upon to make speeches after receiving the bronze plaques recording their deeds on the diamond. Thousands of fans from across the U.S.A. always jam their way into tiny Cooperstown, N.Y., when those Induction Ceremonies are held on midsummer Sunday afternoons.

Naturally enough, Don Drysdale, now a radio and television broadcaster with the Chicago White Sox, put together a carefully written speech to make at his induction. When his Chicago White Sox employers heard that "Big D" was planning to take the Sunday off, however, they were irked and told him straight out that his job status would be seriously jeopardized if he didn't show up for work in the broadcast booth that day as scheduled.

"It was touch and go for a while," said Drysdale. But after Drysdale made an emotional plea to his bosses pointing out that this was a one-in-a-lifetime thing (which, of course, they knew), and after a good bit more wrangling back and forth, he was finally given reluctant permission to travel to Cooperstown for his big day! Strange?

# STRANGE SCHEDULING: OAKLAND PLAYS TWO GAMES IN TWO CITIES ON ONE DAY

For many years the Pacific Coast League season consisted of 200 games or more involving many doubleheaders. The Oakland Oaks played one of the most unusual double-headers ever on April 13, 1913, when they met the Portland Beavers at home for a morning game. Then right after the game with the Beavers, the Oaks sailed across San Francisco Bay to play an afternoon tilt with the San Francisco Seals!

# SUPER FAN MISSED ONLY ONE WORLD SERIES GAME IN 42 YEARS

C. E. "Pat" Olsen, a 6-foot-2-inch righthanded power pitcher, signed a contract with the New York Yankees in 1923 as a 20-year-old and was fully expected by the Yankees to become a star.

For the next five years Olsen labored in the minor league vineyards with stops at Des Moines, Pittsfield and Springfield, Massachusetts, St. Joseph, Missouri, Atlanta, and Amarillo, Texas.

"In 1924, I roomed with Lou Gehrig at the Yankees spring training complex at St. Petersburg, Florida, and thought I was ready at that time to make the big leagues, but I was sent back down to the minors just before the season began," Olsen said recently. "After my last stop with Amarillo of the Western League in 1927, I decided to call it quits as a ballplayer because by that time I knew I wouldn't make it to the majors . . . . Then I got into the oil business in Texas," Olsen added.

Over the years Olsen became an oil millionaire, but his passion for baseball continued unabated. In 1933 he attended the major league's first All-Star Game played at

Chicago's Comiskey Park and from then through 1987 he never missed seeing any of the 58 midsummer classics. He's attended nearly 300 World Series games from 1938 to 1987—in fact, from 1938 until 1980, Pat witnessed 255 consecutive World Series contests, missing the final game of the Kansas City-Philadelphia Series (at Philadelphia) because of a vital business commitment. That's the only Series game he failed to see in nearly 50 years. And he's gone to every Hall of Fame Induction Ceremony at Cooperstown since 1939.

"I doubt very much if any other fan has compiled an attendance record of this magnitude," observed Bob Fishel, Executive Vice President of the American League and a baseball executive with more than 40 years experience.

"I never made more than $300 a month as a minor league player, but once I established myself in business and had the time and resources to travel, I made up my mind not to miss a single one of baseball's premier events," said Pat Olsen.

# BABE'S SIGNATURE WORTH $500, BUT BEWARE! SOME PHONY

It is estimated that Babe Ruth signed at least two million autographs during his lifetime. With only a small fraction of those autographs being extant, values of genuine Ruth signatures are climbing steadily. A Ruth signature on a baseball generally sells for $500 and more.

Collectors should beware, though, because Ruth autographs have been widely counterfeited.

Joe DiMaggio autographs are also in great demand and have substantial value despite the fact that the "Yankee Clipper" is still signing. At an auction conducted at the Oakland-Alameda County Coliseum in conjunction with the July 13, 1987, All-Star game, a Joe DiMaggio autographed baseball was hammered down for $355.

Mel Ott, the Hall of Fame New York Giants home run hitter, didn't mind autographing for fans since his name consists of only six letters. "Master Melvin" got to a point where he could sign 500 autographs per hour.

# ROSTER

Adams, Earl (Sparky), 110
Aguilera, Rick, 106
Aguirre, Hank, 97
Akin, Roy, 37
Alston, Walter (Smokey), 67
Anderson, Bob, 22
Anson, Adrian C. (Cap), 42
Appling, Luke, 36, 63
Ashburn, Richie, 103
Averill, Earl, 24-26, 92

Baker, Del, 19
Banks, Ernie, 22, 89
Bateman, John, 55
Batista, Fulgencio, 39-40
Beck, Walter (Boom Boom), 75-76
Bell, George, 115
Benton, Al, 94-95
Berra, Lawrence (Yogi), 51-52, 59, 118
Bonds, Bobby, 90
Boone, Bob, 54-55
Borst, Bill, 48
Boswell, James, 68
Boudreau, Lou, 23, 60
Bowa, Larry, 34
Bradley, Alva, 23
Bramham, William G., Judge, 73
Bristol, Dave, 65
Brito, Mike, 70
Buhl, Bob, 95, 96

Cain, Bob, 15
Carlisle, Walter, 37
Carson, Al, 37
Castro, Fidel, 39-40
Chapman, Ben, 73
Chapman, Ray, 79
Chozen, Harry, 33-34
Cicotte, Al, 39-40
Clark, Peter P., 117, 118, 119
Clark, Stephen C., 119
Clarkson, John, 46
Cobb, Ty, 10, 38, 77-78, 81, 89

Coleman, Vince, 17-18
Corgan, Chuck, 110
Correll, Vic, 66
Craig, Roger, 28-30
Cramer, Roger (Doc), 38-39
Crawford, Sam, 89
Cross, Jack, 116

Dahlen, William (Bad Bill), 35
Dalkowski, Steve, 71-72
Dark, Alvin, 22
Dauer, Rich, 34
Dean, Jay Hanna (Dizzy), 92
Delmore, Vic, 22
Delsing, Jim, 15
Dickey, Bill, 88
Dietrich, Bill (Bullfrog), 95-96
DiMaggio, Joe, 10, 86-87, 88, 124
Doerr, Bobby, 68
Doubleday, Abner, 119
Drysdale, Don, 120-21
Ducey, Rob, 115
Durocher, Leo, 72
Dykes, Jimmy, 96

Eichhorn, Mark, 85, 91-92
Ennis, Del, 103
Evans, Billy, 33
Evans, Darrell, 10

Feeney, Charles S., 66
Feigner, Eddie, 55
Feller, Bob (Rapid Robert), 13-15, 19, 21, 86, 97
Feller, Marguerite, 13
Feller, Mrs. Bill, 13-15
Fishel, Bob, 123
Fox, Nelson, 118
Foxx, Jimmie, 10-11, 24, 84-85
Frisch, Frankie, 10

Gaedel, Eddie, 15-17
Garner, Phil, 70
Gehrig, Lou, 24, 80, 102, 122
Gehringer, Charlie, 21, 24
Gentile, Jim, 89

125

Gera, Bernice, 26-27
Giamatti, A. Bartlett, 28,
  68-69, 101
Giebell, Floyd, 19, 21
Giles, Warren, 22
Gomez, Vernon (Lefty) (Goofy),
  24, 50-51, 98
Gooden, Dwight, 70, 106
Graves, Abner, 119
Gray, Pete, 48-49
Greenberg, Hank, 20, 94, 114
Grimes, Burleigh, 72-74,
  107-10
Groom, Bob, 105
Grove, Robert Moses (Lefty), 80
Guerra, Carmen, 21

Haas, Eddie, 66
Hallahan, Bill (Wild Bill), 98
Harder, Mel, 84
Harridge, Will, 16
Hart, Mike, 115
Hartnett, Charles Leo (Gabby),
  110
Heath, Jeff, 23
Heathcote, Cliff, 112
Hollocher, Charlie, 112
Hornsby, Rogers, 92-93
Howard, Frank, 91, 93
Huggins, Miller, 102
Hurley, Ed, 16

Jackson, Joe (Shoeless Joe), 88
Jackson, Reggie, 58, 90
Jackson, Vincent Edward (Bo),
  90
James, Dion, 106
John, Tommy, 10
Johnson, Howard, 28-30
Johnson, Samuel, 68
Johnson, Walter, 80, 104-05
Jones, Willie (Puddin' Head),
  103

Kachline, Clifford, 81
Kaufmann, Tony, 111-112
Kilduff, Pete, 108
Killifer, Bill, 112
King, Clyde, 58
Knight, Ray, 106
Krug, Marty, 112
Kuhn, Bowie, 66

Latham, Arlie, 42
LeBourveau, Dewitt (Bevo), 112
Lee, Cliff, 112
Lemon, Bob, 58
Leslie, Roy, 114
Lewis, Franklin, 61
Lindstrom, Fred, 92-93
Linz, Phil, 118
Lipset, Lew, 46-47
Lopez, Al, 54

McDougald, Gil, 92
McGraw, John, 35-36
McGriff, Fred, 115
McGwire, Mark, 95
McKechnie, Bill, 60
Mack, Connie, 36
Mantle, Mickey, 85, 94
Maris, Roger, 54
Martin, Billy, 58, 59, 85
Mattingly, Don, 58, 89-90
Mays, Willie, 10, 11
Metzger, George, 37
Michael, Gene, 58
Miller, Bing, 24
Miller, Lawrence (Hack), 112
Miller, Otto, 108
Mitchell, Dale, 88-89
Mize, Johnny, 87, 118
Mokan, Johnny, 112
Money, Don, 35
Moody, Dwight L., 44, 46
Moore, Charles, 37
Moseby, Lloyd, 115
Mulliniks, Rance, 115
Murcer, Bobby, 58
Musial, Stan, 22, 74, 81

Newsom, Louis Norman (Bobo),
  56
Niekro, Joe, 10
Niekro, Phil, 10
Noeth, LaVerne (Rose), 82

Oh, Sadaharu, 53-54
Ojeda, Bob, 106
Olsen, C. E. (Pat), 122-23
Osborne, Ernie, 112
Ott, Mel, 124
Owen, Marvin, 13
Owens, Jesse, 62

Patkin, Max, 60, 61
Perez, Tony, 10
Pfeffer, Fred, 35
Piersall, Jimmy, 41
Piniella, Lou, 58
Postema, Pam, 27-28
Pottle, F. A., 68
Price, Jackie, 60-61

Ramos, Pedro, 85
Reagan, Ronald, 81
Reichler, Joe, 85
Rickey, Branch, 23, 38, 67
Ring, Jimmy, 111-12
Ripken, Cal, Jr., 80
Ripken, Cal, Sr., 80, 114
Robertson, Sherry, 33
Robinson, Brooks, 91, 93
Robinson, Jackie, 23
Rose, Harry, 81
Rose, Pete, 10, 52-53, 81-83,
   99
Roush, Edd, 30-31
Ruth, George Herman (Babe),
   10, 24, 26, 51, 83-84, 85, 90,
   94, 102, 124
Ryan, Nolan, 10, 70-71, 93

Santana, Rafael, 106
Schott, Marge, 53
Score, Herb, 92
Scott, Everett (Deacon), 102-03
Seedhouse, George E., 59
Sewell, Joe, 77-80
Sisler, George, 38
Smith, Elmer, 108
Speaker, Tris, 37
Staley, Gale, 110
Steinbrenner, George M., III,
   57-59
Stengel, Charles Dillon (Casey),
   72, 75
Stevenson, Robert Louis, 57
Stewart, Harry, 37
Stock, Wes, 97
Strange, Alan (Inky), 47-48

Summers, Bill, 20
Sunday, William Ashley (Billy),
   41-47

Taylor, Sammy, 22
Taylor, Zack, 15, 110
Tebbetts, George (Birdie), 18, 21
Thomassie, Pete, 33
Turner, Robert Edward, III
   (Ted), 64-66

Valenzuela, Fernando, 70
Veeck, Bill, 15-17, 59-62
Vitt, Oscar, 19, 20, 96

Waitkus, Eddie, 103
Walker, Curt, 112
Wambsganss, Bill (Wamby), 108
Warneke, Lon, 67
Washington, Claudell, 32-33,
   91, 93
Weatherly, Roy, 20
Weinert, Phil (Lefty), 112
Whitehill, Earl, 24
Whitt, Ernie, 114
Wilhelm, Hoyt, 10
Wilhelm, Irv (Kaiser), 111-112
Williams, Bob, 73
Williams, Ted, 38-39, 87, 88
Wilson, J. Owen (Chief), 116
Wilson, Lewis R. (Hack), 75-76
Winfield, Dave, 58
Wish, Harvey, 46
Wren, Chris, 27
Wrightstone, Russ, 112
Wynn, Early, 76
Wynn, Early, Jr., 76

Yastrzemski, Carl, 10, 98-99,
   104
Yeager, Steve, 34
York, Rudy, 21
Young, Denton True (Cy),
   117-118
Young, Dick, 101

# GUINNESS
## SPORTS RECORD
## BOOK ·
■■■■■■■■■■■■■

**Featuring**

# 89
**Sports
Games
Pastimes**

*including many minor sports played
in the United States that are not
included in the "GUINNESS
BOOK OF WORLD RECORDS"*

### *Here is what SPORTS ILLUSTRATED had to say about this one-volume all-sports, illustrated encyclopedia:*

"Sports fans, here it is! The ultimate answer book. Everything you have ever wanted to know, needed to know, wondered about in sports—from Guinness, the world's leading record keeper.

"Now you can have at your fingertips literally thousands of facts, figures, names and statistics on every sport of any consequence in the world.

"It's the most valuable sports reference you'll ever own".

*Now completely revised and brought up-to-date*